psalm 130 - p 124 -
words of the Requiem Mass

The Catholic Assembly Book

When we pray, we talk to God: when we
read the divine word, we listen to him.

St Ambrose: *Duties of Ministers*, I.20

The Catholic Assembly Book

James Tolhurst

Gracewing.

Dedicated to The Most Revd Maurice Couve de Murville,
Archbishop of Birmingham

First published in 1996

Gracewing
Fowler Wright Books
2 Southern Ave, Leominster
Herefordshire HR6 0QF

With ecclesiastical approval

ISBN 0 85244 357 9

Typesetting by Action Typesetting Ltd,
Gloucester, GL1 1SP

Printed by Redwood Books,
Trowbridge, Wiltshire, BA14 8RN

Contents

Contents

Foreword

'You must know that there is nothing higher, or stronger, or sounder, or more useful afterwards in life, than some good memory, especially a memory from childhood ... You hear a lot said about education, yet some such beautiful, sacred memory preserved from childhood, is perhaps the best education. If a man stores up many such memories to take into life, then he is saved for his whole life. And even if only one good memory remains with us in our hearts, that alone may serve some day for our salvation.' So speaks Illyusha at the end of Dostoevski's greatest novel, *The Brothers Karamazov*.

Prayer is central to Catholic education, for the whole point of such education is to lead us closer to God. And prayer must be an occasion for storing up as many beautiful memories as possible.

There is no better way to do this than by offering students, in a prayerful setting, the words of sacred scripture. Fr Tolhurst has done us a service by grouping verses from the scriptures under weekly themes, together with short prayers and a saying from the Fathers.

There are many ways in which this helpful resource could be used. For example, the scriptural quotations could fruitfully be taken for daily meditation by teachers and catechists, and verses from the week's selection memorized by teachers and students alike, building up a bank of reference points, of sacred memories, for hope and orientation in later life. It would also be easy to build on what is given here through the use of music and of focal points for prayer and worship related to the weekly themes.

Petroc Willey
Maryvale Institute

Introduction

This book has been designed as a resource work for teachers and leaders of groups in the first place, and then for those who look for assistance in their own private prayer.

The heart of the book consists of five scripture passages for each week, taken from a wide variety of translations for their readability. These are grouped under headings which respond to the call to believe that Jesus is the Son of God and so to find life in his name (John 20.31). This covers the teachings of Christianity, its sacraments, way of life and spiritual conduct (cf. *Catechism of the Catholic Church* no. 2558). These themes are dealt with both in Weeks of the Year (Ordinary time) and in the weeks from Advent to Easter. But the work is drawn up in such a way that passages are interchangeable, using the subject index at the back of the book. If one follows the theme of the sacraments for instance, it could be interrupted with passages from the weeks after Easter.

Some will want to sum up the meeting in their own words, but others may be at a loss, or in a hurry and I have provided two prayers for each week. As a stimulus to meditation or discussion, a short quotation summing up the weekly themes, taken in the main from patristic authors (which I have freely translated), is given at the head of each week. Further material can be found using the index to the *Catechism* at the back. There is an appendix of psalms and prayers and extra material for various feast days and saints days as well as bereavements.

There is a danger that organized prayer can simply become one more 'activity' in the day instead of being the heart of every day. This is perhaps because we have neglected the way in which the scriptures can help us to talk to our heavenly Father by listening to him speaking to us. There are many beautiful thoughts to be found in literature and life generally but there is no substitute for the scriptures. But again the normal size of extracts used in the liturgy are by their nature expansive – for proclamation – whereas traditionally the *Prayer of the Church* has made use of one or two verses to focus our mind and heart. May this book, which makes use of that method deepen our life of prayer. Although it has developed out of my own experience, I have been helped by experts far more knowledgeable than myself, in particular I would mention the late Dom Anselm Rutherford. I am also grateful to Dr Willey, the Editor of *The Sower* for his foreword, and to Andrew Nash and Vincent Sharples for their constructive comments.

James Tolhurst
Edgbaston, 1996

Abbreviations and Acknowledgements

G   *The Psalms, A New Translation*, © 1963, The Grail (England), published by Collins in Fontana Books.

JB/NJB   *The Jerusalem Bible* and *The New Jerusalem Bible*, © 1966, 1985 by Doubleday, a division of Bantam & Doubleday Dell Publishing Group, Inc and Darton, Longman & Todd, Ltd. Used by permission of Doubleday.

K   *The New Testament*, trans. Ronald Knox, © 1945, 1948, 1949, The Catholic Hierarchy of England and Wales, published by Burns Oates and Washbourne.

NEB/REB   *The New English Bible* and *The Revised English Bible*, © 1970, 1989, Oxford and Cambridge University Presses.

RSV/NRSV   Revised Standard Version and New Revised Standard Version, © 1966, 1989, Division of Christian Education of the National Council of the churches of Christ in the United States of America, used by permission.

TEV   *Good News Bible: Today's English Version*, © 1966, 1971 and 1976, American Bible Society, published by The United Bible Societies and Collins/Fount, 1976.

Ordinary Time

Week 1 God revealed in creation

The universe reveals to us the wisdom of the One who maintains it in being.

Gregory of Nyssa: *On the Soul and Resurrection.*

————◁○▷————

1. *Acts 17.24, 25*
   Paul said to the Athenians: 'the God who made the world and everything in it is himself Lord of heaven and earth ... it is he who gives everything – including life and breath – to everyone.'

   JB

2. *Revelation 4.11*
   Our Lord and God! You are worthy to receive glory, honour and power. For you created all things and by your will they were given existence and life.

   TEV

3. *Wisdom 9.1–4*
   God of our ancestors, Lord of mercy, who by your word have made all things, and in your wisdom have fitted man to rule the creatures that have come from you, to govern the world in holiness and justice ...

   JB

4. *Romans 1.20*
   Ever since God created the world this everlasting power and deity – however invisible – have been there for the mind to see in the things he has made.

   JB

5. *Acts 14.15, 17*
Paul and Barnabas said to the people [of Iconium] 'The living God who made sky and earth ... did not leave you without evidence of himself in the good things he does for you.'

NJB

Let us pray:

a) Eternal Father, God of all creation, source of our life, may we praise you by our words and our works. Through Christ our Lord.

b) Lord, you manifest yourself in the wonder of your creation. Grant that we may be worthy of the place in it you have given us. Through Christ our Lord.

Week 2 The response of faith

God, who is all good, has created us and keeps us in being. Everything that happens to us, whether important or insignificant is his concern.

Basil: *Homily 9*

————◦————

1. *Mark 11.22–24*
    Jesus said to his disciples. 'Have faith in God. Truly, I say to you, whoever says to this mountain, "Be taken up and cast into the sea", and does not doubt in his heart, but believes that what he says will come to pass, it will be done for him. Therefore I tell you, whatever you ask in prayer, believe that you receive it, and you will.'

    RSV

2. *Hebrews 13.5–6*
    God himself has said, 'I will not fail you or desert you', and so we can say with confidence, 'With the Lord to help me, I fear nothing ...'

    JB

3. *Romans 8.28*
    We know that all things work together for good for those who love God, who are called according to his purpose.

    NRSV

4. *Matthew 6.31–34*
    Jesus said to his disciples, 'Do not worry, do not say, "What are we to eat? What are we to drink? How are we to be clothed?" It is the pagans who set their hearts on all these things. Your heavenly Father knows you need them all. Set your hearts on his kingdom first, and his right-eousness, and all these other things will be given you as well.

    JB

4

5. *1 Peter 5.6–8*

Humble yourselves under the mighty hand of God, so that he may exalt you in due time. Cast all your anxiety on him, because he cares for you.

NRSV

Let us pray:

a) Almighty God, you govern all things in your wisdom. May we trust you and pray to you for guidance. Through Christ our Lord.

b) Lord God, you know all things. Help us to rest in the certainty of your loving providence. Through Christ our Lord.

Week 3 God speaks to us in revelation

You have studied the holy scriptures, which are true and inspired by the Holy Spirit. You surely know that nothing dishonest or false is written in them.

Clement I: *Letter to the Corinthians*, 45

————◄O►————

1. *2 Timothy 3.16*
   All scripture is inspired by God and can profitably be used for teaching, for refuting error, for guiding people's lives and teaching them to be holy.

   JB

2. *John 14.24*
   Jesus said to the Twelve, 'The word that you hear is not my own: it is the word of the Father who sent me.'

   NJB

3. *Romans 15.4*
   All the words [of scripture] written long ago were written for our instruction; we were to derive hope from that message of endurance and courage which the scriptures bring us.

   K

4. *1 Thessalonians 2.13*
   When you received the word of God [from us] you accepted it not as the word of men but as what it really is, the word of God, which is at work in you believers.

   RSV

5. *Hebrews 2.1–3*

In many and various ways God spoke of old to our fathers by the prophets; but in the last days he has spoken to us by a Son, whom he has appointed the heir of all things, through whom also he created the world.

RSV

Let us pray:

a) Lord God may your word be a light to our lives because it reveals the loving plan of your salvation. Through Christ our Lord.

b) Eternal Father may we listen to your holy word with reverence and proclaim it by our living faith. Through Christ our Lord.

Week 4 God speaks to us in his Son

He who walked among us as man, brought all things into being as the Word, who dwells continually with the Father as his eternal Son.

Athanasius: *On the Incarnation*, 17

━━━◄o►━━━

1. *Matthew 11.27*
   Jesus declared, 'All things have been delivered to me by my Father; and no one knows the Son except the Father; and no one knows the Father except the Son and those to whom the Son chooses to reveal him.'

   RSV

2. *John 1.1–3*
   In the beginning was the Word: the Word was with God and the Word was God. He was with God in the beginning. Through him all things came to be, not one thing had its being but through him. All that came to be had life in him ...

   JB

3. *John 1.18*
   No one has ever seen God; it is the only Son, who is nearest to the Father's heart, who has made him known.

   JB

4. *John 17.8*
   Jesus raised his eyes to heaven and said, 'I have given them the teaching you gave to me, and they have truly accepted this, that I came from you, and have believed that it was you who sent me.'

   JB

5. *John 8.28*

Jesus said to the crowd, '... I do nothing of myself: what the Father has taught me is what I preach; he who sent me is with me, and has not left me to myself for I always do what pleases him.'

JB

Let us pray:

a) Lord, you are the source of all wisdom. Direct our thoughts, words and actions through Christ your Son who lives and reigns for ever and ever

b) Almighty God, you have given us in your Son, the way, the truth and the life. May we be enlightened by his words and come to share his life. Through Christ our Lord.

Week 5 'In the Image of God'

Recognise your natural dignity! Remember that image of God in which you were created, for even if it has been defaced in Adam, it has been restored in Christ.

Leo I: *7th Homily on the Nativity*, 6

————◄○►————

1. *Psalm 8.4–6*
   What is man that you should spare a thought for him, the son of man that you should care for him? Yet you have made him little less than a god, you have crowned him with glory and splendour, made him lord over the work of your hands, set all things under his feet.

   JB

2. *Mark 8.36–38*
   Jesus said to his disciples and to the crowd, 'How is a man the better for it, if he gains the whole world at the expense of losing his own soul? For a man's soul, what price can be high enough?'

   K

3. *Ephesians 1.5*
   He destined us in love to be his sons through Jesus Christ, according to the purpose of his will, to the praise of his glorious grace which he freely bestowed on us ...

   RSV

4. *Colossians 3.10*
   You have put on a new self which will progress towards true knowledge the more it is renewed in the image of its Creator.

   NJB

10

5. *Romans 8.29*

All those who from the first were known to him, he has destined from the first to be moulded into the image of his Son.

K

Let us pray:

a) Almighty Father, author of all life, may we respect the sanctity of every human being from the first moment of his existence to his last. Through Christ our Lord

b) Eternal God, we confess that you have made us in your image so that we can always remember you, think of you and love you. Through Christ our Lord.

Week 6 God speaks in our conscience

If our conscience tells us to do something and we follow it, we keep it alive. But if we go against it again and again we gradually smother it and in the end it will no longer let itself be heard.

Dorotheus of Gaza: *Teachings*, 3

———◄o►———

1. *1 John 1.5–7*
   This is what we have heard from him and are declaring to you: God is light, and there is no darkness in him at all. If we say that we share in God's life while we are living in darkness, we are lying, because we are not living the truth.

   NJB

2. *Ephesians 5.8–10*
   You yourselves used to be in the darkness, but since you have become the Lord's people, you are in the light. So you must live like people who belong to the light, for it is the light that brings a rich harvest of every kind of goodness, righteousness and truth.

   TEV

3. *John 3.19*
   Jesus said to Nicodemus, 'Though the light has come into the world, men have shown they prefer darkness to light because their deeds were evil. And indeed, everybody who does wrong hates the light and avoids it, for fear his actions should be exposed; but the man who lives by the truth comes out into the light ...'

   JB

4. *1 Peter 2.15–17*
It is God's will that by doing right you should put to silence the ignorance of foolish men. Live as free men, yet without using your freedom as a pretext for evil; but live as servants of God.

RSV

5. *1 John 3.21*
If we cannot be condemned by our own conscience, we need not be afraid in God's presence, and whatever we ask him, we shall receive, because we keep his commandments.

JB

Let us pray:

a) Merciful Father, strengthen our conscience that we may be aware of the presence of God speaking to us and informing us of his laws. Through Christ our Lord.

b) Give us grace, all powerful God, to avoid all occasions of sin and to use them as opportunities of overcoming our weakness out of love for you. Through Christ our Lord

Week 7 The tragedy of original sin

In Adam our human nature sinned because sin was transmitted to all
his descendants through this one man's sin.

Ambrose: *Defence of the Prophet David*, 2

———◁◦▷———

1. *1 Corinthians 15.22–24*
    Just as all die in Adam, so in Christ all will be brought to
    life; but all of them in their proper order: Christ the first-
    fruits, and next, at his coming, those who belong to him.

    NJB

2. *Romans 5.15*
    If it is certain that through one man's fall so many died, it is
    even more certain that divine grace, coming through the
    one man, Jesus Christ, came to so many as an abundant free
    gift.

    JB

3. *Romans 7.14–16*
    We are well aware that the Law is spiritual; but I am a crea-
    ture of flesh and blood sold as a slave to sin. I do not
    understand my own behaviour; I do not act as I mean to,
    but I do things that I hate. While I am acting as I do not
    want to, I still acknowledge the Law is good, so it is not
    myself acting, but the sin which lives in me.

    NJB

4. *Romans 8.12–14*
    There is no necessity for us to obey our unspiritual selves or
    to live unspiritual lives. If you do live in that way, you are
    doomed to die; but if by the Spirit you put an end to the
    misdeeds of the body you will live.

    JB

14

5. *Romans 5.18–20*

   As one man's fall brought condemnation on everyone, so the good act of one man brings everyone life and makes them justified. As by one man's disobedience many were made sinners, so by one man's obedience many will be made righteous.

   JB

Let us pray:

a) Heavenly Father may the light of your truth take away the darkness from our lives so that we may serve you in true freedom. Through Christ our Lord.

b) Lord God, we ask you that desires which come from your inspiration may not be altered by any temptation. Through Christ our Lord.

Week 8 God the Holy Spirit

He is the source of all holiness; he enlightens every mind that seeks after truth.

Basil: *On the Holy Spirit*, 8

———◄○►———

1. *Romans 8.15–18*
    When we cry, 'Abba! Father!' it is the Spirit himself bearing witness with our spirit that we are children of God, and if children, then heirs, heirs of God and fellow heirs with Christ, provided we suffer with him in order that we may also be glorified with him.

    RSV

2. *1 Corinthians 2.10–12*
    The Spirit reaches the depths of everything, even the depths of God. After all, the depths of a man can only be known by his own spirit, not by any other man, and in the same way the depths of God can only be known by the Spirit of God.

    JB

3. *Romans 8.26*
    The Spirit too comes to help us in our weakness. For when we cannot choose words in order to pray properly, the Spirit himself expresses our plea in a way that could never be put into words, and God who knows everything in our hearts knows perfectly well what he means, and that the pleas of the saints expressed by the Spirit are according to the mind of God.

    JB

16

4. *John 16.23–25*
Jesus said to his disciples, 'I tell you most solemnly anything you ask for from the Father he will grant in my name. Until now you have not asked for anything in my name. Ask and you will receive, and so your joy will be complete.

JB

5. *Ephesians 1.13–14*
In him you also, who have heard the word of truth ... and have believed in him, were sealed with the promised Holy Spirit, which is the guarantee of our inheritance ...

RSV

Let us pray:

a) Almighty God, you guide the hearts of all who believe, to the light of your truth by the gift of your Spirit. May we rejoice in the true wisdom which he brings to us. Through Christ our Lord.

b) Eternal Father you send to us the Spirit who is the love you share with your Son. May we be filled with that love and share it with our neighbour. Through Christ our Lord.

Week 9 Prayer: our conversation with God

You should not think of prayer as being merely a matter of words. It is a desire for God, a devotion that cannot be described, which does not come from ourselves, but is the gift of God's grace.

John Chrysostom: *On Prayer*, 6

———◁◊▷———

1. *Matthew 6.5–7*
   Jesus said to the crowd, 'When you pray, you must not be like the hypocrites; for they love to stand and pray ... that they may be seen by men. Truly I say to you, they have received their reward. But when you pray, go into your room and shut the door and pray to your Father who is in secret; and your Father who sees in secret will reward you.'

   RSV

2. *Jeremiah 29.12–14*
   The Lord God says, 'When you call to me, and come to plead with me, I will listen to you. When you seek me you shall find me, if you seek me with all your heart.'

   JB

3. *Matthew 6.7–9*
   Jesus said to his disciples 'In your prayers do not babble as the pagans do, for they think that by using many words they will make themselves heard. Do not be like them; your Father knows what you need before you ask him.'

   JB

4. *Matthew 18.19–20*
   Jesus said to his disciples, 'If two of you on earth agree to ask anything at all, it will be granted to you by my Father in heaven. For where two or three meet in my name, I shall be there with them.'

   JB

5. *Matthew 7.7–8*

Jesus said to his disciples, 'Ask, and it will be given you; seek, and you will find; knock, and it will be opened to you. For every one who asks receives, and he who seeks finds, and to him who knocks it will be opened.'

RSV

Let us pray:

a) Almighty and eternal God, hear the prayers of your people and grant that what we ask for in faith, we may obtain. Through Christ our Lord.

b) Everlasting Father, May we believe that you are always present and that you see and know us. May we turn to you in prayer every day of our lives. Through Christ our Lord.

Week 10 The Church: a living communion in Christ

(cf. Easter 6)

Just as the power of the holy flesh of Christ binds together those who receive it into one body, so in the same way, the one undivided Spirit of God who lives in all, draws all into a spiritual unity.

Cyril of Alexandria: *Commentary on John*, 11

———◄◊►———

1. *John 15.4–6*
   Jesus said to his disciples, 'Abide in me, and I in you. As the branch cannot bear fruit by itself unless it abides in the vine, neither can you, unless you abide in me. I am the vine, you are the branches. He who abides in me, and I in him, he it is that bears much fruit, for apart from me you can do nothing.'

   RSV

2. *John 17.21*
   Jesus prayed, 'Father may they be one in us, as you are in me and I am in you, so that the world may believe it was you who sent me.'

   JB

3. *1 John 2.28*
   Abide in him, so that when he appears we may have confidence and not shrink from him in shame at his coming. If you know that he is righteous, you may be sure that every one who does right is born of him.

   RSV

4. *Acts 2.44–46*
   All who believed were together and had all things in common; and they sold their possessions and goods and distributed them to all, as any had need.

   RSV

20

5. *Ephesians 4.15–17*

If we live by the truth and in love, we shall grow up in all ways into Christ, who is the head, by whom the whole body is fitted and joined together ... until it has built itself up, in love.

JB

Let us pray:

a) Almighty Father, you gather together those you have made followers of your Son. Keep them so united by your grace that the splendour of your Church may be seen by all. Through Christ our Lord.

b) Everlasting God, break down the division between Christians so that we may serve you in faith and love and come to worship you in spirit and truth. Through Christ our Lord.

Week 11 The bishops, successors of the apostles

We bishops who lead the Church must above all hold and defend this unity so that we can show how the episcopal authority is one and undivided.

Cyprian: *The Unity of the Catholic Church*, 4

———◁◦▷———

1. *John 10.14–16*
   Jesus said to the crowd, 'I am the good shepherd; I know my own and my own know me, just as the Father knows me and I know the Father; and I lay down my life for my sheep.'

   JB

2. *Matthew 16.18–20*
   Jesus said to Simon, 'I tell you, you are Peter, and on this rock I will build my church, and the powers of death shall not prevail against it. I will give you the keys of the kingdom of heaven, and whatever you bind on earth shall be bound in heaven, and whatever you loose on earth shall be loosed in heaven.'

   RSV

3. *Luke 22.28–31*
   Jesus said to the Twelve, 'You are the men who have stood by me faithfully in my trials; and now I confer a kingdom on you, just as my Father conferred one on me ... you will sit on thrones to judge the twelve tribes of Israel.'

   NJB

4. *Acts 20.28*
   Paul said to the elders of the church, 'Keep watch, then, over yourselves, and over God's Church, in which the Holy

22

Spirit has made you bishops; you are to be the shepherds of that flock which he won for himself at the price of his own blood.'

K

5. *1 Peter 5.2, 3*
Be the shepherds of the flock of God that is entrusted to you: watch over it ... Never be a dictator over any group that is put in your charge, but be an example that the whole flock can follow.

JB

Let us pray:

a) Eternal Father you have built your Church on the foundation of the apostles. May your people be strengthened in the unity of the faith by their successors, the Pope and the bishops. Through Christ our Lord.

b) Almighty God, grant that your bishops, the successors of the apostles may unite the Church in one communion, bearing witness to you. Through Christ our Lord.

Week 12 The grace of Christ

We have risen again ... we have been justified .... All of this St Paul calls an abundant free gift, showing that what we have received is not just a cure for the wounds which have been inflicted by our sins, but health and splendour and dignity, glory and honour, far in excess of what is natural to us.

John Chrysostom: *On the Letter to the Romans*, 10

————◁◦▷————

1. *John 10.12*
   Jesus said to the crowd, 'I have come so that they may have life and have it to the full.'

   JB

2. *Ephesians 1.3–5*
   Blessed be the God and Father of our Lord Jesus Christ, who has blessed us with all the spiritual blessings of heaven in Christ. Before the world was made, he chose us, chose us in Christ, to be holy and spotless, and to live through love in his presence.

   JB

3. *John 1.16–18*
   From his fulness we have all received, grace upon grace. The law indeed was given through Moses; grace and truth came through Jesus Christ.

   NRSV

4. *Phil 2.13*
   It is God who, for his own generous purpose, gives you the intention and the powers to act.

   NJB

24

5. *John 1.4*

In him was life and the life was the light of men. The light shines in the darkness and the darkness has not overcome it.

RSV

Let us pray:

a) Renew us almighty Father with that grace which perfects in us the image of your Son. Through Christ our Lord

b) Eternal Father, live in us always, as you live in your beloved Son with the Holy Spirit. Through the same Christ our Lord.

Week 13 Baptism

(cf. Easter 2)

Baptism is the seal of eternal life and of rebirth in God, so that we are not just the children of mortal parents, but also the children of the eternal and unchangeable God.

Irenaeus: *Presentation of the Apostolic Preaching*, 3

————◄O►————

1. *Matthew 3.16–17*
   As Jesus was baptized he came up from the water, and suddenly the heavens opened and he saw the Spirit of God descending like a dove and coming down on him. And a voice spoke from heaven, 'This is my Son, the Beloved; my favour rests on him.'

   JB

2. *John 3.5–7*
   Jesus said to Nicodemus, 'Truly, truly, I say to you, unless one is born of water and the Spirit, he cannot enter the kingdom of God. That which is born of the flesh is flesh, and that which is born of the Spirit is spirit.'

   RSV

3. *Titus 3.5*
   He saved us, not because of any works of righteousness that we had done, but according to his mercy, through the water of rebirth and renewal by the Holy Spirit.

   NRSV

4. *Galations 3.26–28*
   All of you are the children of God, through faith, in Christ Jesus, since every one of you that has been baptized has been clothed in Christ.

   NJB

26

5. *Ephesians 5.25–28*
Christ loved the Church and sacrificed himself for her to make her holy. He made her clean by washing her in water with a form of words, so that when he took her to himself she would be glorious ... holy and faultless.

JB

Let us pray:

a)   Eternal Father, may we who have become members of your family on earth come to share in the communion of your saints in heaven. Through Christ our Lord.

b)   Merciful Father, may all who have been renewed in the likeness of your Son turn from their sins to serve you in the midst of your holy people. Through Christ our Lord.

Week 14 Confirmation

(cf. Week 8)

God the Father has marked you with his sign, Christ our Lord has confirmed you and has placed his pledge, the Spirit, in your heart.

Ambrose: *On the Mysteries*, 7

———◄○►———

1. *Acts 8.14–18*
   When the apostles in Jerusalem heard that Samaria had accepted the word of God, they sent Peter and John to them, and they went down there and prayed for them to receive the Holy Spirit, for ... they had only been baptized in the name of the Lord Jesus. Then they laid their hands on them and they received the Holy Spirit.

   NJB

2. *Galations 5.22–24*
   The fruit of the Spirit is love, joy, peace, patience, kindness, goodness, faithfulness, gentleness, self-control; against such there is no law.

   RSV

3. *1 Corinthians 12.12–14*
   Just as a human body, though it is made up of many parts, is a single unit because all these parts, though many, make one body, so it is with Christ. In the one Spirit we were all baptized, Jews as well as Greeks, slaves as well as citizens, and one Spirit was given to us all to drink.

   JB

4. *1 Corinthians 12.4–8*
   There are varieties of gifts, but the same Spirit; and there are varieties of service, but the same Lord; and there are vari-

28

ieties of working, but it is the same God who inspires them all in every one. To each is given the manifestation of the Spirit for the common good.

RSV

5. *Romans 8.14–15*
Everyone moved by the Spirit is a son of God. The spirit you received is not the spirit of slaves bringing fear into your lives again; it is the spirit of sons.

Let us pray:

a) Grant eternal Father that those whom you have made your own, may, through the holiness of their lives be a clear sign of your kingdom in the world. Through Christ our Lord.

b) Eternal Father, grant us by the gift of your Holy Spirit that we may be truly wise, and with his power strengthen our weakness. Through Christ our Lord.

Week 15 The Eucharist: Body and Blood of Christ

(cf. Corpus Christi)

For no one will be in Christ, unless Christ is in him; unless he has taken into himself the flesh of Christ who took human flesh.

Hilary of Poitiers: *On the Trinity*, 8

————◁◦▷————

1. *John 6.48–52*

   Jesus said to the Jews, 'I am the bread of life. Your fathers ate the manna in the wilderness, and they died. This is the bread which comes down from heaven, that a man may eat of it and not die. I am the living bread which came down-fromheaven; if any one eats of this bread, he will live for ever; and the bread which I shall give for the life of the world is my flesh.

   RSV

2. *1 Corinthians 11.23–26*

   This is what I received from the Lord, and in turn passed on to you: that on the same night that he was betrayed, the Lord Jesus took some bread, and thanked God for it, and he said, 'This is my body, which is for you; do this as a memorial of me.' In the same way he took the cup after supper, and said, 'This cup is the new covenant in my blood. Whenever you drink it, do this as a memorial of me.'

   JB

3. *1 Corinthians 10.16–18*

   The cup of blessing which we bless, is it not a participation in the blood of Christ? The bread which we break, is it not a participation in the body of Christ? Because there is one bread, we who are many are one body, for we all partake of the one bread.

RSV

4. *John 6.57–59*
Jesus said to the Jews 'As the living Father sent me, and I live because of the Father, so he who eats me will live because of me. This is the bread which came down from heaven, not such as the fathers ate and died; he who eats this bread will live for ever.'

RSV

5. *John 6.53*
Jesus said to the Jews, 'Truly I say to you, unless you eat the flesh of the Son of man and drink his blood, you have no life in you.'

RSV

Let us pray:

a) Almighty God, grant that we who receive the Body and Blood of your Son may become sharers in his divinity. Through Christ our Lord.

b) Merciful Father, through the mystery of your Body and Blood grant to your Church peace and unity according to your will. Through Christ our Lord.

Week 16 The Eucharist: sacrifice of praise

It is not the priest who is responsible for the offerings being transformed into Christ's body and blood; it is Christ himself, who was crucified for us.

> John Chrysostom: *On the Treachery of Judas*, 1

———◁◦▷———

1. *Romans 12.1–3*
   I implore you by God's mercy to offer your very selves to him; a living sacrifice, dedicated and fit for his acceptance, the worship offered by mind and heart. Adapt yourselves no longer to the pattern of this present world, but let your minds be remade and your whole nature thus transformed. Then you will be able to discern the will of God, and to know what is good, acceptable, and perfect.

   NEB

2. *Hebrews 7.26–28*
   It was fitting that we should have such a high priest, holy, blameless, unstained, separated from sinners, exalted above the heavens. He has no need, like those high priests, to offer sacrifices daily, first for his own sins and then for those of the people; he did this once for all when he offered up himself.

   RSV

3. *Matthew 5.23–25*
   Jesus said to the crowd, 'So if you are offering your gift at the altar, and there remember that your brother has something against you, leave your gift there before the altar and go; first be reconciled to your brother, and then come and offer your gift.'

   RSV

4. *1 Peter 2.4–6*
Come to him, to that living stone, rejected by men but in God's sight chosen and precious; and like living stones be yourselves built into a spiritual house, to be a holy priest-hood, to offer spiritual sacrifices acceptable to God through Jesus Christ.

RSV

5. *Hebrews 10.10*
It is by God's will that we have been sanctified through the offering of the body of Jesus Christ once for all.

NRSV

Let us pray:

a) Almighty God may we offer you the sacrifice which your beloved Son made upon the cross which he now renews upon the altar. Through Christ our Lord.

b) Eternal Father, may we so reverence the sacred mysteries of the Body and Blood of your Son that we may always enjoy the fruit of the redemption. Through Christ our Lord.

Week 17 Penance and reconciliation

(cf. Lent 3)

It is necessary to confess our sins to those who are the stewards of God's mysteries.

Basil: *Brief Rules*, n. 288

———————◄○►———————

1. *Psalm 32.5*
   I said: 'I will confess my offence to the Lord.' And you, Lord, have forgiven the guilt of my sin.

   G

2. *John 20.22–24*
   Jesus said to his disciples, 'Receive the Holy Spirit. For those whose sins you forgive, they are forgiven; for those whose sins you retain, they are retained.'

   JB

3. *Matthew 9.4–8*
   Jesus said to the scribes, 'Which of these is easier: to say, "Your sins are forgiven" or to say, "Get up and walk"? But to prove to you that the Son of man has authority on earth to forgive sins' – he said to the paralytic – 'get up, and pick up your bed and go home.' And the man got up and went home.

   JB

4. *Luke 7.47*
   Jesus said to Simon the Pharisee, 'I tell you that her sins, many as they are, have been forgiven her, because she has shown such great love. It is someone who is forgiven little who shows little love.'

   NJB

5. *1 John 1.8–10*
   If we say we have no sin in us, we are deceiving ourselves
   and refusing to admit the truth; but if we acknowledge our
   sins, then God who is faithful and just will forgive our sins
   and purify us from everything that is wrong.

JB

Let us pray:

a) Almighty Father, through the Sacrament of Penance may
   the good we do and the evil we endure, heal our sins and
   help us to grow in holiness. Through Christ our Lord.

b) Merciful God come to the aid of those who are burdened
   by their sins, so that they may rejoice in the remedy which
   your Sacrament provides. Through Christ our Lord.

Week 18 Anointing of the sick

Brethren, whoever is sick, come quickly to the Church, to receive health of body and deserve to obtain forgiveness of sins.

Caesarius of Arles: *Homily 265*

————◄o►————

1. *James 5.14–16*
   Is any among you sick? Let him call for the elders of the church, and let them pray over him, anointing him with oil in the name of the Lord: and the prayer of faith will save the sick man, and the Lord will raise him up; and if he has committed any sins, he will be forgiven.

   RSV

2. *Matthew 18.12*
   Jesus said to his disciples, 'Tell me, suppose a man has a hundred sheep and one of them strays; will he not leave the ninety-nine on the hillside and go in search of the stray? I tell you solemnly, if he finds it, it gives him more joy than do the ninety-nine that did not stray at all.'

   JB

3. *Matthew 11.28–30*
   Jesus exclaimed, 'Come to me, all you who labour and are overburdened, and I will give you rest. Shoulder my yoke and learn from me, for I am gentle and humble in heart, and you will find rest for your souls. Yes, my yoke is easy and my burden light.'

   JB

4. *Mark 2.17*
   Jesus said to the scribes, 'It is not the healthy who need the doctor, but the sick. I did not come to call the virtuous, but sinners.'

   JB

5. *Matthew 8.17*
Jesus healed all that were sick, in fulfilment of the word spoken by Isaiah the prophet, 'He took our infirmities upon himself, and bore our sicknesses'.

K

Let us pray:

a) Lord God you are the source of all health. Come to raise up those who are sick, that they may serve you in this world, and one day meet you in heaven. Through Christ our Lord.

b) Almighty Father, may we share with you that compassion which your Son showed for the sick, that we may obtain mercy and forgiveness for our weakness. Through Christ our Lord.

Week 19 Holy Orders

We should bear in mind that the bishop and his clergy are like Aaron and his sons. As there is only one Temple and one Lord, so there should be only one Ministry.

Jerome: *Letter to Nepotianus*

◁○▷

1. *John 15.15–17*
   Jesus said to the Twelve, 'No longer do I call you servants, for the servant does not know what his master is doing; but I have called you friends, for all that I have heard from my Father I have made known to you. You did not choose me, but I chose you and appointed you that you should go and bear fruit and that your fruit should abide ...'

   RSV

2. *Mark 10.29–31*
   Jesus said to his disciples, 'I tell you solemnly, there is no one who has left house, brothers, sisters, father, children or land for my sake and for the sake of the gospel who will not be repaid a hundred times over, houses, brothers, sisters, mothers, children and land – not without persecution – now in this present time, and, in the world to come, eternal life.'

   JB

3. *John 20.21–22*
   Jesus said to his disciples 'As the Father sent me, so am I sending you.' After saying this he breathed on them and said, 'Receive the Holy Spirit.'

   JB

4. *2 Timothy 1.6*

I remind you, Timothy, to rekindle the gift of God that is within you through the laying on of my hands; for God did not give us a spirit of timidity but a spirit of power and love and self-control.

RSV

5. *Hebrews 5.1–5*

Every high priest chosen from among men is appointed to act on their behalf in relation to God, to offer gifts and sacrifices for sins ... And one does not take the honour upon himself, but he is called by God, just as Aaron was.

RSV

Let us pray:

a) Eternal God, choose those in holy orders to be the dispensers of your holy mysteries. Keep them faithful to the sacraments which they give to your people and strengthen them by the words which they preach. Through Christ our Lord.

b) Father, you choose those in orders to serve, after the example of your beloved Son. May they be filled with his love to give themselves as he did. Through Christ our Lord.

Week 20 Marriage

Certainly it is God who joins two into one, so that when God marries a woman to a man, they are no longer two; and since God joins them he gives a grace to those who are so united.
Origen: *Commentary on Matthew*, 14

————◄○►————

1. *Mark 10.6–10*
   Jesus said to the Pharisees, 'From the beginning of creation God made them male and female. This is why a man must leave father and mother and the two become one body. They are no longer two, therefore, but one body. So then, what God has united, man must not divide.'

   JB

2. *1 Corinthians 6.19–20*
   Your body is the temple of the Holy Spirit, who is in you and whom you received from God. You are not your own property, then; you have been bought at a price. So use your body for the glory of God.

   NJB

3. *Ephesians 5.21–25*
   Be subject to one another out of reverence for Christ. Wives, be subject to your husbands, as to the Lord. For the husband is the head of the wife as Christ is the head of the church ... Husbands love your wives, as Christ loved the church and gave himself up for her ...

   RSV

4. *1 Corinthiams 7.3*
   The husband must give his wife what she has the right to expect, and so to the wife to the husband. The wife has no rights over her own body; it is the husband who has them.

40

In the same way, the husband has no rights over his body:
the wife has them.

JB

5. *Ephesians 5.28*
    Husbands must love their wives as they love their own
    bodies; for a man to love his wife is for him to love himself.
    A man never hates his own body ... and that is the way
    Christ treats the Church, because it is his body and we are
    its living parts.

JB

Let us pray:

a) God our Father, source of all life, give the grace of being
    good parents to those you have joined in the power of your
    sacrament. Through Christ our Lord.

b) Merciful Father, may those who give themselves to each
    other in marriage, bear witness in their lives to the love of
    Christ who joins them together. Through the same Christ
    our Lord.

Week 21 The Commandments: Law of God

Human beings are worthy of receiving laws from God since they possess reason and have knowledge and intelligence and can work within the bounds of freedom in obedience to God who has subjected all things to them.

Tertullian: *Against Marcion*, 2

————◄o►————

1. *Matthew 5.17*
   Jesus said to his disciples, 'Think not that I have come to abolish the law and the prophets; I have come not to abolish them but to fulfil them. For truly, I say to you, till heaven and earth pass away, not an iota, not a dot, will pass from the law until all is accomplished.'

   RSV

2. *Romans 2.13–15*
   It is not listening to the Law but keeping it that will make people holy in the sight of God ... Pagans who have never heard of the Law but are led by reason to do what the Law command ... can point to the substance of the Law engraved on their hearts.

   JB

3. *John 14.21*
   Jesus said to the Twelve, 'Anybody who receives my commandments and keeps them will be one who loves me; and anybody who loves me will be loved by my Father, and I shall love him and show myself to him.'

   JB

4. *Matthew 5.19*
   Jesus said to his disciples, 'Anyone who infringes even one of the least of these commandments and teaches others to

42

do the same will be considered least in the kingdom of heaven; but the person who keeps them and teaches them will be considered great in the kingdom of heaven.'

NJB

5. *Matthew 7.21*
Jesus said to the crowds, 'It is not those who say to me, "Lord, Lord", who will enter the kingdom of heaven, but the person who does the will of my Father in heaven.'

JB

Let us pray:

a)   Merciful Father, deliver us from our sins so that we can faithfully carry out the commandments of your law. Through Christ our Lord.

b)   Almighty God, open our hearts to your commandments so that we may conform our will to yours. Through Christ our Lord.

Week 22 The Commandments: love of God, love of neighbour

The good we do to our neighbour, the Lord receives as if it was done to himself.

Basil: *Homily on Psalm 48*

———◄○►———

1. *Matthew 5.43–46*
Jesus said to the crowd, 'You have heard that it was said, "You shall love your neighbour and hate your enemy". But I say to you, love your enemies and pray for those who persecute you, so that you may be sons of your Father who is in heaven; for he makes his sun rise on the evil and the good, and sends rain on the just and on the unjust.'

RSV

2. *John 13.34*
Jesus said to the Twelve, 'I give you a new commandment: love one another; just as I have loved you.'

JB

3. *1 John 5.3–5*
This is what loving God is – keeping his commandments; and his commandments are not difficult, because anyone who has been begotten by God has already overcome the world; this is the victory over the world – our faith.

JB

4. *1 John 2.3–5*
By this we may be sure that we know him, if we keep his commandments. He who says 'I know him' but disobeys his commandments is a liar, and the truth is not in him; but

44

whoever keeps his word, in him truly love for God is perfected.

RSV

5. *1 John 4.20*
   Anyone who says, 'I love God', and hates his brother, is a liar, since a man who does not love the brother that he can see cannot love God, whom he has never seen.

JB

Let us pray:

a) Merciful Father, May the Church be a living sign of your love by the charity we show to our neighbour. Through Christ our Lord.

b) May we be one in mind and heart by a single faith and a living charity. Through Christ our Lord.

Week 23 Sunday, the Lord's Day of rest

We meet together in common assembly on the Sun's Day because it is the first day on which God ... created the world, and on which Christ our Saviour rose from the dead.

Justin: *First Apology*, 67

◄○►

1. *Luke 4.16*
   Jesus came to Nazareth, where he had been brought up; and he went to the synagogue, as his custom was, on the sabbath day.

   RSV

2. *Deuteronomy 5.12–14*
   Observe the sabbath day and keep it holy, as the Lord your God commanded you. Six days you shall labour and do all your work. But the seventh day is a sabbath to the Lord your God.

   NRSV

3. *Isaiah 58.13*
   If you call the sabbath a delight and the holy day of the Lord honourable; if you honour it, not going your own ways, serving your own interests ... then you shall take delight in the Lord.

   NRSV

4. *Hebrews 4.9–11*
   There must still be, therefore, a seventh-day rest reserved for God's people, since to enter the place of rest is to rest after your work, as God did after his.

   NJB

5. *Colossians 3.17*
Whatever you do, in word or deed, do everything in the name of the Lord Jesus, giving thanks to God the Father through him.

RSV

Let us pray:

a) Lord God, give us a constant fear and love of your holy name, that we may honour you on the day which you made holy by the resurrection of your Son. Through Christ our Lord.

b) Heavenly Father, as living stones built up into a temple to your glory, let us offer you fitting praise in the Church's worship. Through Christ our Lord.

Week 24 Reverencing God in our words

Let us keep ourselves free from all backbiting and slander; let us seek to justify ourselves by deeds not merely by words.

Clement: *Letter to the Corinthians, 30*

————◁◦▷————

1. *James 1.22–26*
   You must do what the word tells you, and not just listen to it and deceive yourselves. To listen to the word and not obey it, is like looking at your own features in a mirror, and then, after a quick look, going off immediately forgetting what you looked like. But the man who looks steadily at the perfect law of freedom and makes that his habit ... will be blessed in every undertaking.

   JB

2. *James 5.12*
   Do not swear by heaven or by the earth, or use any oaths at all. If you mean 'yes', you must say 'yes'; if you mean 'no', say 'no'. Otherwise you make yourselves liable to judgement.

   JB

3. *Matthew 23.20–23*
   Jesus said to his disciples, 'Someone who swears by the altar is swearing by that and by everything on it. And someone who swears by the Temple is swearing by that and by the One who dwells in it.'

   NJB

4. *James 1.19–20*
   Remember this ... be quick to listen but slow to speak and slow to rouse your temper. God's righteousness is never served by man's anger.

   JB

5. *Ephesians 4.24*
   Put on the new nature created in God's likeness, which shows itself in the upright and devout life called for by the truth.

REB

Let us pray:

a) Merciful Father through the example of patience given to us by your Son, may we be conscious of the harm which our words may do. Through Christ our Lord.

b) Almighty God, may we always be willing to find excuses for our neighbour, aware as we are of our own weakness. Through Christ our Lord.

Week 25 Truthfulness

It is a difficult and rare virtue, to mean what we say, to love without dissimulation, to think no evil, to bear no grudge, to be free from self-ishness, to be innocent and straightforward. This character of mind is something far above the generality of people; and when realised in due measure, one of the surest marks of Christ's elect.

J. H. Newman: *Parochial and Plain Sermons*, Volume 2, 27

---◄○►---

1. *John 1.6–8*
   A man came, sent by God. His name was John. He came as a witness, to bear witness to the light, so that everyone might believe through him.

   NJB

2. *John 8.12*
   Jesus spoke to the people, 'I am the light of the world; anyone who follows me will not be walking in the dark; he will have the light of life.'

   JB

3. *John 18.37*
   Jesus answered Pilate, 'You say that I am a king. For this I was born, and for this I have come into the world, to bear witness to the truth. Every one who is of the truth hears my voice.'

   RSV

4. *1 Peter 2.1*
   Rid yourselves, then, of all spite, deceit, hypocrisy, envy and carping criticism.

   NJB

5. *Ephesians 4.25*
   So from now on there must be no more lies. Speak the truth to one another, since we are all parts of one another.

   NJB

Let us pray:

a) Merciful God, heal us of the dishonesty that injures our relationships with each other, and grant us the courage to speak the truth. Through Christ our Lord.

b) Heavenly Father, may we live up to the example set us by your Son in all that we say and do. Through the same Christ our Lord.

Week 26 Peace not war

To set nothing before the love of Christ; not to give way to anger; not to wait for an opportunity to get angry; not to keep deceit in one's heart; not to make a treacherous peace.

Benedict: *Rule 4*

————◄○►————

1. *Ephesians 4, 2–5*
    Bear with one another charitably, in complete selflessness, gentleness and patience. Do all you can to preserve the unity of the Spirit by the peace that binds you together. There is one Body, one Spirit, just as you were all called into one and the same hope when you were called.

    JB

2. *Hebrews 12.14–16*
    Pursue peace with everyone; and the holiness without which no one will see the Lord. See to it that no one fails to obtain the grace of God; that no root of bitterness springs up and causes trouble ...

    NRSV

3. *James 3.17*
    The wisdom which comes down from above is essentially something pure; it also makes for peace, and is kindly and considerate; it is full of compassion and shows itself by doing good; nor is there any trace of partiality or hypocrisy in it. Peacemakers, when they work for peace, sow the seeds which will bear fruit in holiness.

    JB

4. *1 John 2.9–11*
    He who says he is in the light and hates his brother is in the darkness still. He who loves his brother abides in the light ...

    RSV

52

5. *Matthew 5.9*

Jesus said to the crowd and his disciples, 'Blessed are the peacemakers, for they will be called children of God.'

NRSV

Let us pray:

a) Eternal God source of all harmony, give us that peace which the world cannot give so that we may put away our hatred and forgive even as you forgive us. Through Christ our Lord.

b) Heavenly Father, support all who work to avert war so that they may achieve true peace based on justice and respect for the value of human life. Through Christ our Lord.

Week 27 Helping those in need

(cf. Week 22)

By all means spend money on your house, but do not lose sight of your brother who is in need – he is a temple of far greater value.

John Chrysostom: *Homily on Matthew*, 50

———◁◯▷———

1.   *James 2.15–17*
If one of the brothers or one the sisters is in need of clothes and has not enough food to live on, and one of you says to them, 'I wish you well; keep yourself warm and eat plenty', without giving them these bare necessities of life, then what good is that?

NJB

2.   *Matthew 25.37–41*
Then the righteous will answer him, 'Lord, when did we see you hungry and feed you, or thirsty and give you to drink? And when did we see you a stranger and welcome you, or naked and clothe you? And when did we see you sick or in prison and visit you?' And the King will answer them, 'Truly I say to you, as you did it to one of the least of these my brethren, you did it to me.'

RSV

3.   *1 Peter 4.8–11*
Above all, never let your love for each other grow insincere, since love covers over many a sin. Welcome each other into your houses without grumbling. Each one of you has received a special grace, so, like good stewards responsible for all these different graces of God, put yourselves at the service of others.

JB

4. *1 John 3.17–19*
If any one has the world's good and sees his brother in need, yet closes his heart against him, how does God's love abide in him? Little children, let us not love in word or speech but in deed and in truth.

RSV

5. *2 Corinthians 9.8*
God ... will make sure that you will always have all you need for yourselves in every possible circumstance, and still have something to spare for all sorts of good work.

JB

Let us pray:

a) Lord, make us worthy to serve those who live and die in poverty and hunger throughout our world, seeing you in them. Through Christ our Lord.

b) Heavenly Father, may we never separate our love of you from the charity we show to our neighbour. Through Christ our Lord.

Week 28 Bearing true witness

(cf. Easter 3)

We can only teach the truth to our neighbour if our own life matches
the message we preach ... If our life bears witness to our words.

Clement of Alexandria: *Miscellaneous Studies*, 7

————◄○►————

1. *Matthew 10.32*
    Jesus said to his disciples, 'Every one who acknowledges me
    before men, I also will acknowledge before my Father who
    is in heaven; but whoever denies me before men, I also will
    deny before my Father who is in heaven.'

    RSV

2. *John 8, 31–33*
    Jesus said to the Jews who believed in him, 'If you continue
    in my word, you are truly my disciples, and you will know
    the truth, and the truth will make you free.'

    RSV

3. *2 Timothy 2.11–14*
    Here is a saying that you can rely on: If we have died with
    him, then we shall live with him. If we hold firm, then we
    shall reign with him. If we disown him, then he will disown
    us. We may be unfaithful, but he is always faithful, for he
    cannot disown his own self.

    JB

4. *1 Corinthians 4.5*
    There must be no passing of premature judgement. Leave
    that until the Lord comes: he will light up all that is hidden
    in the dark and reveal the secret intentions of men's hearts.

Then will be the time for each one to have whatever praise he deserves, from God.

JB

5. *1 John 4.14–16*
We ourselves saw and we testify tht the Father sent his Son as saviour of the world. If anyone acknowledges that Jesus is the Son of God, God lives in him and he in God.

JB

Let us pray:

a) Almighty God, through the gift of your Holy Spirit, ground us in your truth and keep us blameless in your service. Through Christ our Lord.

b) All powerful God may we be inspired by the example of your only Son who came on earth to bear witness to the truth. Through Christ our Lord.

Week 29 The use of power

One in authority should judge himself ruthlessly but be kind and merciful in the judgements he passes on those subject to him.

John Chrysostom: *Homily on Matthew*, 72

———◄○►———

1. *Romans 13.1*
    Let every person be subject to the governing authorities. For there is no authority except from God, and those that exist have been instituted by God.

    RSV

2. *Romans 13.7*
    Pay every man, then his due; taxes, if it be taxes, revenue, if it be revenue; respect and honour, if it be respect and honour. Do not let anybody have a claim on you, except the claim which binds us to love one another.

    K

3. *Matthew 10.24*
    Jesus said to the Twelve, 'The disciple is not superior to his teacher, nor the slave to his master. It is enough for the disciple that he should grow to be like his teacher, and the slave like his master.'

    JB

4. *Matthew 20.25*
    Jesus called the Twelve to him and said, 'You know that among the pagans, the rulers lord it over them, and their great men make their authority felt. This is not to happen among you ... Anyone who wants to be great among you must be your servant ... just as the Son of Man came not to be served but to serve, and to give his life as a ransom for many.'

    JB

5. *Matthew 23.11–12*
    Jesus said to the people and his disciples, 'The greatest
    among you must be your servant. Anyone who exalts
    himself will be humbled, and anyone who humbles himself
    will be exalted.'

    JB

Let us pray:

a) Lord God, give us a constant fear and love of your holy
    name, for you never cease to govern those whom you
    found on the basis of your love. Through Christ our Lord.

b) Almighty Father, may we do everything for your glory, and
    in fulfilment of your will. Through Christ our Lord.

Week 30 The pure in heart

There may be those who hear me who are caught up in their sinful and impure habits and feel ashamed, and are told 'If you go on like that you will come to a bad end'. They reply 'We cannot quit the habit'. I ask the Lord to raise them up, because he is life, he is resurrection.

Augustine: *Homily on John*, 29

◀◎▶

1. *Mark 7.20–24*
   Jesus said to his disciples, 'It is what comes out of a man that makes him unclean. For it is from within, from men's hearts, that evil intentions emerge: fornication, theft, murder, adultery, avarice, malice, deceit, indecency, envy, slander, pride, folly. All these evil things come from within and make a man unclean.'

   JB

2. *Matthew 5.27*
   Jesus said to the crowd, 'You have learnt how it was said, "You must not commit adultery". But I say this to you: if a man looks at a woman lustfully, he has already committed adultery with her in his heart.'

   JB

3. *1 Thessalonians 4.3*
   This is the will of God, your sanctification; that you abstain from unchastity; that each one of your know how to control his own body in holiness and honour ...

   RSV

4. *Philippians 4.8*
    All that is true, all that is noble, all tht is just and pure, all
    that is lovable and attractive, whatever is excellent and
    admirable – fill your thoughts with these things.

    REB

5. *1 John 3.3*
    Surely everyone who entertains this hope must purify
    himself, must try to be as pure as Christ.

    JB

Let us pray:

a) Merciful Father cleanse us from all impurity of mind and
    body, that we may be worthy of the work to which you call
    us. Through Christ our Lord.

b) Heavenly Father, grant that by subduing our unworthy
    desires, we may learn to love the inspirations you wish to
    give us. Through Christ our Lord.

Week 31 'He was rich but he became poor'

Avarice normally dulls our senses and distorts our judgements so that we come to regard riches as the reward of virtue.

Ambrose: *Letter to Constantius*

1. *Luke 16.10–12*
   Jesus said to his disciples, 'The man who can be trusted in little things can be trusted in great; the man who is dishonest in little things will be dishonest in great. If then you cannot be trusted with money, that tainted thing, who will trust you with genuine riches?'

   JB

2. *Luke 12.15*
   Jesus said to a man in the crowd, 'Be on your guard against avarice of any kind, for life does not consist in possessions, even when someone has more than he needs.'

   NJB

3. *1 Timothy 6.7–10*
   We brought nothing into the world, and we can take nothing out of it; but as long as we have food and clothing, let us be content with that. People who long to be rich are a prey to temptation; they get trapped into all sorts of foolish and dangerous ambitions which eventually plunge them into ruin and destruction.

   JB

4. *2 Corinthians 8.9*
   Remember how generous the Lord Jesus was: he was rich, but he became poor for your sake, to make you rich out of his poverty.

   JB

5. *Acts 4.32*
The group of believers was one in mind and heart. No one said that any of his belongings were his own but they all shared with one another everything they had.

TEV

Let us pray:

a) Lord, teach us to be honest with what we have and what we handle for others, so that we may be worthy to serve you. Through Christ our Lord.

b) Heavenly Father, may we use our possessions wisely and not allow them to separate us from your love. Through Christ our Lord.

Week 32 Death, the final journey

(cf. Funerals)

Death is not the final destination but an interruption on the way. Once
our journey on earth is ended, we continue on to eternity.

Cyprian: *Treatise on death*, 16

———◁○▷———

1. *1 John 2.15–17*
Do not love the world or the things in the world. The love
of the Father is not in those who love the world ... And the
world and its desire are passing away, but those who do the
will of God live forever.

NRSV

2. *1 Thessalonians 4.13–15*
We want you to be quite certain ... about those who have
fallen asleep, to make sure that you do not grieve for them,
as others do who have no hope. We believe that Jesus died
and rose again, and that in the same way God will bring
with him those who have fallen asleep in Jesus.

NJB

3. *2 Corinthians 5.1*
We know that when the tent we live in – our body here on
earth – is torn down, God will have a house in heaven for
us to live in, a home he himself has made, which will last for
ever.

TEV

4. *2 Timothy 4.7–9*
I have run the race to the finish: I have kept the faith; all there is to come now is the crown of righteousness reserved for me; which the Lord, the righteous judge, will give to me on that Day; and not only to me but to all those who have longed for his Appearing.

JB

5. *John 14.2–3*
Jesus said to his apostles, 'In my Father's house are many rooms ... And when I go and prepare a place for you, I will come again and take you to myself, that where I am you may be also.'

RSV

Let us pray:

a) Merciful Father, help us to watch in prayer at all times so that we may be be ready to welcome you at our last hour. Through Christ our Lord.

b) Almighty God, as I came from you, as I am made by you, as I live in you, so may I at last return to you and be with you for ever. Through Christ our Lord.

Week 33 The resurrection of the body

The perfection of the redemption in those who have been filled with grace, is not only to see the face of God but to rise again to everlasting life, honour and glory.

Ambrose: *Letter to Eusebius*

1. *Romans 6.8–12*
   If we have died with Christ, we believe that we shall also live with him. For we know that Christ being raised from the dead will never die again; death no longer has dominion over him. The death he died he died to sin, once for all, but the life he lives, he lives to God. So you must also consider yourselves dead to sin but alive to God in Christ Jesus.

   RSV

2. *John 6.39*
   Jesus said to the crowd, 'The will of him who sent me is that I should lose nothing of all that he has given to me, and that I should raise it up on the last day.'

   JB

3. *1 Corinthians 15.42–44*
   With the resurrection of the dead ... what is sown unhonoured, rises in glory; what is sown in weakness, is raised in power.

   K

4. *Philippians 3.20*
   The Lord Jesus Christ ... will change our weak mortal bodies and make them like his own glorious body, using that power by which he is able to bring all things under his rule.

   TEV

5. *John 11.25*
   Jesus said to Martha, 'I am the resurrection. If anyone believes in me, even though he dies he will live, and whoever lives and believes in me will never die.'

   TEV

Let us pray:

a) God our Father, we believe in the death and resurrection of your Son. May those who have died come to share in the glory that he has won for them. Through Christ our Lord.

b) Eternal God, through your Son, those who have died pass from death to life. Give them the pardon which they have always desired so that they can come with joy to the happiness you have prepared for them. Through Christ our Lord.

Week 34 He will come to judge

He will come at the last day, not in human weakness but in the glory that belongs to him as God and king with his holy angels.

Cyril of Alexandria: Against Nestorius, 4

———◁O▷———

1. *Acts 17.31*
   Paul said to the Athenians, 'God ... has fixed a day when the whole world will be judged in uprightness by a man he has appointed. And God has publicly proved this by raising him from the dead.'

   NJB

2. *Acts 10.41–43*
   Peter addressed Cornelius, 'We are those witnesses – we have eaten and drunk with Jesus after his resurrection from the dead – and he has ordered us to proclaim this to his people and to tell them that God has appointed him to judge everyone, alive or dead.'

   JB

3. *John 5.24*
   Jesus said to the crowd, 'I tell you most solemnly, whoever listens to my words, and believes in the one who sent me, has eternal life; without being brought to judgement he has passed from death to life.'

   JB

4. *Luke 6.36–38*
   Jesus said to the crowds, 'Be compassionate as your Father is compassionate. Do not judge and you will not be judged; do not condemn, and you will not be condemned; forgive and you will be forgiven.'

   JB

5. *John 12.47–49*
Jesus declared publicly: 'I have come not to condemn the world, but to save the world: he who rejects me and refuses my words has his judge already: the word itself that I have spoken will be his judge on the last day.'

JB

Let us pray:

a) Heavenly Father prepare us for that final meeting with your Son who is our king and our judge. Through Christ our Lord.

b) Almighty God, to whom all time belongs and all the ages; may we put our trust in your final judgement. Through Christ our Lord.

Advent

—◆◇◆—

Advent 1 Thy kingdom come

In the evening of your life they will examine you in love. Learn to love God as God wishes to be loved.

John of the Cross: Sayings, n. 57

————◄○►————

1. *Luke 21.34ff*
    Jesus said to his disciples, 'Watch yourselves ... [for] that day will be sprung on you suddenly, like a trap ... Stay awake, praying at all times, for the strength to survive all that is going to happen, and to stand with confidence before the Son of man.'

    JB

2. *Luke 21.25, 27–28*
    Jesus said to his disciples, 'There will be signs in the sun and moon and stars ... and they will see the Son of man coming in a cloud with power and great glory. When these things begin to take place, look up and raise your heads high, because your redemption is near at hand.'

    JB

3. *Matthew 24.42–45*
    Jesus said to his disciples. 'If the householder had known in what part of the night the thief was coming, he would have watched and would not have let his house be broken into. Therefore you also must be ready; for the Son of man is coming at an hour you do not expect.'

    RSV

4. *Romans 8.17–19*
    If we are children [of God] we are heirs as well: heirs of God and coheirs with Christ, sharing his sufferings so as to share his glory. I think that what we suffer in this life can

72

never be compared to the glory, as yet unrevealed which is waiting for us.

5. *Luke 23.43*
    The other criminal said to Jesus, 'Remember me when you come into your kingdom.' 'Indeed, I promise you,' he replied 'Today you will be with me in paradise.'

    JB

Let us pray:

a) Heavenly Father, may we confess that there is no other name other than your Son's by which we may be saved, and so give glory to you. Through Christ our Lord.

b) Almighty God, may we see in your Son the promised Saviour and desire to inherit the kingdom prepared for us. Through Christ our Lord.

Advent 2 The promised Saviour

The prophets spoke in a way which looked forward to Christ, but the
Gospel fulfils their message once and for all.

Ignatius of Antioch: *Letter to the Philadelphians*, 9

―――◄○►―――

1. *John 1.26–28*
   John said to the priests and Levites, 'I baptise with water;
   but there stands among you – unknown to you – the one
   who is coming after me; and I am not fit to undo his sandal-
   strap.'

   JB

2. *Luke 7.16*
   The people glorified God saying, 'A great prophet has arisen
   among us' and 'God has visited his people'.

   RSV

3. *Luke 24.44*
   Jesus said to the Twelve, 'These are my words that I spoke
   to you while I was still with you – that everything written
   about me in the law of Moses, the prophets, and the psalms
   must be fulfilled.'

   NRSV

4. *Luke 10.24*
   Jesus said to his disciples, 'Many prophets and kings wanted
   to see what you see, and never saw it; to hear what you
   hear, and never heard it.'

   NJB

5. *Acts 10.43*
To him all the prophets bear witness that everyone who believes in him receives forgiveness of sins through his name.

RSV

Let us pray:

a) Almighty Father, send us your Holy Spirit that we may recognize your Son as our Saviour. Through the same Christ our Lord.

b) Heavenly Father, may we praise you for giving us a fulfilment of our hope, and make us lead lives worthy of you. Through Christ our Lord.

Advent 3 A Virgin shall conceive

(cf. Feasts of Our Lady)

The reason why ... the Son of God became the Son of man was that man, being united to the Word would receive divine sonship.

Irenaeus: *Against the Heresies*, Book 3, 19

————◄○►————

1. *Luke 1.31–34*
   The angel said to Mary, 'Behold you will conceive in your womb and bear a son, and you shall call his name Jesus. He will be great, and will be called the Son of the Most High; and the Lord God will give to him the throne of his father David, and he will reign over the house of Jacob for ever; and of his kingdom there will be no end.'

   RSV

2. *Luke 1.35*
   The angel said to Mary, 'The Holy Spirit will come upon you and the power of the Most High will cover you with its shadow. And so the child will be holy and will be called Son of God.'

   JB

3. *Isaiah 9.6*
   For there is a child born for us, a son given to us and dominion is laid on his shoulders; and this is the name they give him: Wonder-Counsellor, Mighty-God, Eternal-Father, Prince-of-Peace. Wide is his dominion in a peace that has no end.

   JB

4. *Galatians 4.4*
    When the appointed time came, God sent his Son, born of
    a woman, born a subject to the Law, to redeem the subjects
    of the Law and to enable us to be adopted as sons.

    JB

5. *Philippians 2.10*
    At the name of Jesus every knee should bow, in heaven and
    on earth ... and every tongue confess that Jesus Christ is
    Lord, to the glory of God the Father.

    RSV

Let us pray:

a) Merciful Father, forgive the weakness of your servants and
    save us through the powerful intercession of the Mother of
    your Son. Through Christ our Lord.

b) Eternal Father, may we glorify you in your Son who is your
    very presence and power. Through the same Christ our
    Lord.

Advent 4 A Saviour is born to us

You are firmly convinced about our Lord, who is truly of David's race according to the flesh, and Son of God according to the power of God, truly born of a virgin.

Ignatius of Antioch: *Letter to the Smyrnaeans*, 1

——◄◦►——

1. *Micah 5.2*
   But you, [Bethlehem] Ephrathah, the least of the clans of Judah, out of you will be born for me the one who is to rule over Israel; his origin goes back to the distant past, to the days of old.

   JB

2. *Luke 1.42–46*
   Elizabeth gave a loud cry and said, 'Of all women you are the most blessed, and blessed is the fruit of your womb. Why should I be honoured with a visit from the mother of my Lord? For the moment your greeting reached my ears, the child in my womb leapt for joy. Yes, blessed is she who believed that the promise made her by the Lord would be fulfilled.'

   JB

3. *Luke 2.6–8*
   The time came for Mary to have her child, and she gave birth to a son, her first-born. She wrapped him in swaddling clothes, and laid him in a manger because there was no room for them at the inn.

   JB

4. *Luke 2.8–12*

    In that region there were shepherds out in the field, keeping watch over their flock by night. And an angel of the Lord appeared to them, and glory of the Lord shone around them, and they were filled with fear. And the angel said to them, 'Be not afraid; for behold, I bring you news of great joy which will come to all the people, for to you is born this day in the city of David, a Saviour, who is Christ the Lord.'

    RSV

5. *Luke 2.16–20*

    The shepherds went with haste and found Mary and Joseph and the child lying in the manger. When they saw this they made known what had been told them about this child; and all who heard it were amazed at what the shepherds told them. But Mary treasured all these words and pondered them in her heart.

    NRSV

Let us pray:

a) Grant us, Lord God that we may imitate in our lives your Son, who for our sake humbled himself to share our humanity. Through Christ our Lord.

b) Almighty God, through the incarnation of your Son you have given humanity grace, life and the hope of eternity; may we live so to be worthy of so great a gift. Through Christ our Lord.

Epiphany

The magi were prompted to leave their own country and to set out on a weary journey not only because of the light of the star but also because of that inner light by which God drew them on to know and love him.

John Chrysostom: *Homily on Matthew*, 8

————◁○▷————

1. *Matthew 2.1–3*
When Jesus was born in Bethlehem of Judea in the days of Herod the king, behold wise men from the East came to Jerusalem, saying, 'Where is he who has been born king of the Jews? For we have seen his star in the East, and have come to worship him.'

RSV

2. *Matthew 2, 11*
And going into the house they saw the child with his mother Mary, and falling to their knees they did him homage. Then, opening their treasures, they offered him gifts of gold and frankincense and myrrh.

JB

Let us pray:

a) Lord God, may we who have been brought to know you as the one true God, always be faithful to the light of your inspirations. Through Christ our Lord.

b) Eternal God may your word be taken to the ends of the earth, so that all nations may come to walk in the light of your truth. Through Christ our Lord.

80

Lent

Ash Wednesday

We should put more emphasis on cutting down on our faults than on cutting down on our food.

Leo I: *Homily 6 On Lent*, 2

———◄○►———

1. *Matthew 6.1*
   Jesus said to his disciples, 'Be careful not to parade your good deeds before men to attract their notice; by doing this you will lose all reward from your Father in heaven.'

   JB

2. *Hebrews 12.1–2*
   Let us also lay aside every weight, and sin which clings so closely, and let us run with perseverance the race that is set before us, looking to Jesus the pioneer and perfecter of our faith ...

   RSV

Let us pray:

a) Heavenly Father make our following of your Son during this season of Lent, holy through our self-denial. Through Christ our Lord.

b) Merciful God, you have shown us a greater love in the life and death of your Son. May we be generous ourselves during this Lent to those in need. Through Christ our Lord.

Lent 1 God tempts no one

As pilgrims on a journey, our life cannot be without temptation, for only through temptation can we progress in virtue and come to know ourselves ... We notice that Christ underwent temptation but *not* that he overcame it. See yourselves tempted in him and overcoming the temptation also in him.

Augustine: *Exposition of Psalm 60*

————◄○►————

1. *James 1.13*
   let no one say when he is tempted, 'I am tempted by God';
   for God cannot be tempted with evil and he tempts no one;
   but each person is tempted when he is lured and enticed by
   his own desire.

   RSV

2. *1 Corinthians 10.13*
   God is faithful, and he will not let you be tempted beyond
   your strength, but with the temptation will also provide the
   way of escape, that you may be able to endure it.

   RSV

3. *Deuteronomy 8.17–19*
   Beware of saying in your heart, 'My own strength and the
   might of my own hand won this power for me'. Remember
   the Lord your God: it was he who gave you this strength
   and won you this power.

   JB

4. *Matthew 26.40–42*

Jesus said to Peter, 'So, could you not watch with me one hour? Watch and pray that you may not enter into temptation; the spirit indeed is willing, but the flesh is weak.'

RSV

5. *Luke 22.31–33*

Jesus said to Simon, 'Satan has got his wish to sift you all like wheat; but I have prayed for you, Simon, that your faith may not fail, and once you have recovered, you in your turn must strengthen your brothers.'

NJB

Let us pray:

a) Everliving God, help us to fight against temptations of body and soul, by the example and grace of your beloved Son. Through the same Christ our Lord.

b) Almighty God, may we trust always in your power and not in our own efforts to overcome any temptation. Through Christ our Lord.

Lent 2 He was transfigured

Jesus reveals the splendour of his hidden glory ... so that the members of the Church may look forward to the glory that has already shone forth in his transfiguration.

Leo 1: Homily on the Transfiguration, 3

————◁◉▷————

1. *Luke 9.28–32*
   Jesus took with him Peter and John and James and went up the mountain to pray. As he prayed, the aspect of his face was changed and his clothing became brilliant as lightning. Suddenly there were two men there talking to him; they were Moses and Elijah appearing in glory, and they were speaking of his passing which he was to accomplish in Jerusalem.

   JB

2. *2 Corinthians 3.18*
   We all see as in a mirror to glory of the Lord, and we are being transformed into his likeness with ever increasing glory.

   REB

3. *2 Peter 1.16–18*
   We had seen his majesty with our own eyes. He was honoured and glorified by God the Father, when a voice came to him ... This is my Son, the Beloved; he enjoys my favour.

   NJB

4. *Colossians 1.26–27*
   The mystery that has been hidden throughout the ages ... but has now been revealed to his saints ... this mystery, which is Christ in you, the hope of glory.

   NRSV

5. *1 Timothy 3.16*
The mystery of our religion is very deep indeed: He was made visible in the flesh, justified .in the Spirit, seen by angels, proclaimed to the gentiles, believed in throughout the world, taken up in glory.

NJB

Let us pray:

a) Almighty Father, who in the mystery of the glorious trans-figuration of your Son, confirmed our adoption as your children, grant that we may become worthy of such a dignity. Through Christ our Lord.

b) Heavenly Father, enlighten us who have been filled with your light at our baptism, so that we may always walk in your light. Through Christ our Lord.

Lent 3 Forgive us our trespasses

(cf. Week 17)

Nothing makes us resemble God more than always to be able to forgive.

John Chrysostom: *Homily on Matthew*, 61

———◄○►———

1. **Luke 17.3**
   Jesus said to his disciples, 'If your brother does some thing wrong, reprove him and, if he is sorry, forgive him. And if he wrongs you seven times a day and seven times comes back to you and says, "I am sorry", you must forgive him.'

   JB

2. **Colossians 3.13**
   Bear with one another; forgive each other as soon as a quarrel begins. The Lord has forgiven you; now you must do the same.

   JB

3. **Luke 6.35**
   Jesus said to the crowd, 'Love your enemies and do good, and lend without any hope of return. You will have a great reward, and you will be sons of the Most High, for he himself is kind to the ungrateful and the wicked.'

   JB

4. **James 5.19**
   If one of you wanders from the truth, and some one brings him back, he may be sure tht anyone who can bring back a sinner from the error of his way will save his own soul from death and will cover a multitude of sins.

   RSV

5. *Matthew 6.14*
Jesus said to the crowd, 'If you forgive others the wrongs they have done, your heavenly Father will also forgive you.'

REB

Let us pray:

a) Merciful God, give to the good what their goodness deserves, and to sinners the forgiveness that their sorrow has gained. Through Christ our Lord.

b) Merciful God help us to recognise our faults and the pain that they bring to others. Through Christ our Lord.

Lent 4 Jesus our redeemer

The Lord who was delivered up to death for us and had such pity for us, is alone able to forgive us for the sins we have committed against him.

Cyprian: *On the Lapsed*, 17

—◄o►—

1. *Ephesians 1.7*
   In christ we have redemption through his blood, the forgiveness of our trespasses, according to the riches of his grace that he lavished on us.

   NRSV

2. *Luke 1.67*
   Zechariah said, 'Blessed be the Lord God of Israel, for he has visited and redeemed his people.'

   RSV

3. *Luke 24.26*
   Jesus said to the two disciples, 'Was it not necessary that the Christ should suffer and so enter into his glory?'

   NJB

4. *Matthew 20.27–29*
   Jesus said to his apostles, 'Anyone who wants to be first among you must be your slave, just as the Son of Man came not to be served but to serve, and to give his life as a ransom for many.'

   JB

5. *1 John 2.1–3*
   If any one does sin, we have an advocate with the Father,
   Jesus Christ the righteous; and he is the expiation for our
   sins, and not for ours only but also for the sins of the whole
   world.

RSV

Let us pray

a)   Lord our God, your Son gave himself up for love of us.
   May we always rely on the power of his redemption in the
   sacraments of the Church. Through Christ our Lord.

b)   All powerful God, obtain for us that freedom from our sins
   and that fulness of forgiveness which comes from your
   mercy. Through Christ our Lord.

Lent 5 The language of the cross

(cf. Feasts of Saints)

If you wish to imitate Simon of Cyrene, take up your cross and follow our Lord.

Gregory Nazianzen: *Dissertation*, 45

———◁○▷———

1. *1 Corinthians 1.18–20*
   The language of the cross may be illogical to those who are not on the way to salvation, but those of us who are on the way see it as God's power to save. As scripture says, 'I shall destroy the wisdom of the wise and bring to nothing all the learning of the learned'.

   JB

2. *Ephesians 5.1–3*
   Try then, to imitate God, as children of his that he loves, and follow Christ by loving as he loved you, giving himself up in our place as a fragrant offering and a sacrifice to God.

   JB

3. *Galatians 2.20*
   I have been crucified with Christ; it is no longer I who live but Christ who lives in me; and the life I now live in the flesh, I live by faith in the Son of God, who loved me and gave himself for me.

   RSV

4. *Mark 8.34–36*

Jesus called the people and his disciples to him and said, 'If anyone wants to be a follower of mine, let him renounce himself and take up his cross and follow me. For anyone who wants to save his life will lose it; but anyone who loses his life for my sake, and for the sake of the gospel, will save it.'

JB

5. *Romans 8.18*

I consider that the sufferings of this present time are not worth comparing with the glory that is to be revealed to us.

RSV

Let us pray:

a) Merciful God, grant through the merits of your Son's passion and death that we may amend our lives by true repentance. Through Christ our Lord.

b) Almighty God, may we humble ourselves so that we can exalt you. May we die to ourselves so as to live to you. Through Christ our Lord.

Holy Week He has laid down his life for us

If you would truly worship the passion of Christ, you must see it in such a way that you are suffering in him.

Leo I: Homily on the Passion, 15

---

1. *John 13.1*
   Now before the feast of the Passover, when Jesus knew that the hour had come to depart out of this world to the Father, having loved his own who were in the world, he loved them to the end.

   RSV

2. *Matthew 26.20–24*
   When evening came he was at table with the twelve disciples. And while they were eating, he said, 'I tell you solemnly, one of you is about to betray me.' They were greatly distressed and started asking him in turn, 'Not I, Lord, surely?' He answered, 'Someone who has dipped his hand into the dish with me, will betray me.'

   JB

3. *Matthew 26,.36–40*
   Jesus then came with his disciples to a place called Gethsemane. He took with him Peter and the two sons of Zebedee. Distress and anguish overwhelmed him, and he said to them, 'My heart is ready to break with grief. Stop here, and stay awake with me.' Then he went on a little farther and prayed, 'My Father, if it is possible, let this cup pass me by. Yet not my will but yours.'

   REB

4. *Mark 15.21*
They compelled a passer-by, Simon of Cyrene, who was coming in from the country, the father of Alexander and Rufus, to carry his cross. And they brought him to the place called Golgotha (which means the place of a skull).

RSV

5. *1 Peter 2.21, 24*
Christ suffered for you and left you an example for you to follow the way he took ... He was bearing our faults in his own body on the cross, so that we might die to our faults and live for holiness; through his wounds you have been healed.

JB

Let us pray:

a) Lord, protect your people, by the sign of the holy cross, so that they may always renounce sin and do penance for it. Through Christ our Lord.

b) Heavenly Father, have mercy on us in our weakness, for the sake of the blood which your Son shed on the cross. Through the same Christ our Lord.

Paschal time

Easter 1 Faith in the risen Christ

Thomas saw one thing and believed another. Divinity could not be seen with mortal eyes; and so seeing a man, he confesses God ... exclaiming that he is the God that he cannot see.

Gregory I: *On the Judgement and the Resurrection*, 8

————◀◉▶————

1. *1 Corinthians 15.16–18*
   If the dead are not raised, then Christ has not been raised. If Christ has not been raised, your faith is futile and you are still in your sins.

   NRSV

2. *1 Timothy 6.11–13*
   You must aim to be upright and religious, filled with faith and love, perseverance and gentleness. Fight the good fight of faith and win the eternal life to which you were called and for which you made your noble profession of faith ...

   NJB

3. *John 20.28–30*
   Thomas said to Jesus, 'My Lord and my God'. Jesus replied, 'You believe because you can see me. Happy are those who have not seen and yet believe.'

   JB

4. *2 Corinthians 4.13*
   We too believe and therefore we, too, speak, realizing that he who raised up the Lord Jesus will raise us up with Jesus in our turn, and bring us to himself ...

   NJB

5. *Romans 10.9*

If you confess with your lips that Jesus is Lord and believe in your heart that God raised him from the dead, you will be saved.

RSV

Let us pray:

a) Eternal Father, live in me always, as you always live in your beloved Son who conquered death itself. Through Christ our Lord.

b) Almighty God, grant to us who believe in your Son, truly risen from the dead, an even stronger faith. Through Christ our Lord.

Easter 2 Dying and rising in Christ

We died with him in order to be made clean. We rose again with him because we were glorified with him.

Gregory of Nazianzus: *Homily on Baptism*, 9

———◄○►———

1. *Romans 6.4*
   When we were baptized we went into the tomb with him and joined hin in death, so that as Christ was raised from the death by the Father's glory, we too might live a new life.

   JB

2. *Colossians 2.12*
   You have been buried with him, when you were baptized; and by baptism, too, you have been raised up with him through your belief in the power of God who raised him from the dead.

   JB

3. *Matthew 28.19*
   Jesus said to the eleven, 'Go therefore and make disciples of all nations, baptizing them in the name of the Father and of the Son and of the Holy Spirit, teaching them to observe all that I have commanded you ...'

   RSV

4. *1 Peter 3.21*
   Baptism ... now saves you, not as a removal of dirt from the body but as an appeal to God for a clear conscience, through the resurrection of Jesus Christ.

   RSV

5. *Romans 8.11*

   If the Spirit of him who raised Jesus from the dead dwells in you, he who raised Christ from the dead will give life to your mortal bodies also through his Spirit that dwells in you.

   NRSV

Let us pray:

a) Almighty God, in baptism we died with Christ and rose with him. May we always acknowledge before men the name of him through whom we are reborn again to you. Through Christ our Lord.

b) Lord God give us the wisdom and the strength to be worthy followers of your Son who conquered sin and death. Through the same Christ our Lord.

Easter 3 The lay apostolate

(cf. Week 28)

The Lord is not content with only interior belief but rather asks of us
an outward confession of our faith, encouraging us to a greater confidence and a deeper love.

John Chrysostom: *Homily on Matthew,* 35

———◄○►———

1. *Matthew 25.34–37, 39*
   Then the king will say to those on his right hand, 'Come,
   you whom my Father has blessed, take for your heritage the
   kingdom prepared for you since the foundation of the
   world. For I was hungry and you gave me food; I was
   thirsty and you gave me drink; I was a stranger and you
   made me welcome; naked and you clothed me, sick and
   you visited me, in prision and you came to see me ... as
   you did this is to one of the least of these brothers of mine,
   you did it to me.'

   JB

2. *1 Peter 3.15–17*
   Reverence the Lord Christ in your hearts, and always have
   your answer ready for people who ask you the reason for
   the hope that you all have. But give it with courtesy and
   respect and with a clear conscience, so that those who
   slander you when you are living a good life in Christ may
   be proved wrong in the accusations that they bring.

   JB

3. *Matthew 5.14–17*
   Jesus said to his disciples, 'You are the light of the world. A
   city built on a hill-top cannot be hidden. No one lights a lamp
   to put it under a tub; they put it on a lamp-stand where it

shines for everyone in the house. In the same way your light must shine in the sight of men, so that, seeing your good works, they may give the praise to your Father in heaven.'

JB

4. *Colossians 3.23*
Whatever you do, work at it with all your heart, as though you were working for the Lord and not for men. Remember that the Lord will give you as a reward what he has kept for his people. For Christ is the real master you serve.

TEV

5. *1 Corinthians 15.58*
Never admit defeat; keep on working at the Lord's work always, knowing that, in the Lord, you cannot be labouring in vain.

JB

Let us pray:

a) Eternal Father, you have called us to co-operate in your plan of creation. May our work help to make this world a more just and loving place for all. Through Christ our Lord.

b) Eternal God, may we who have been enlightened by Christ help others to come to his light. Through the same Christ our Lord.

Easter 4 The call to holiness

Our aim must be our own perfection; but our perfection is Christ himself.

Augustine: *Exposition of Psalm 55*

————◀◦▶————

1. *Matthew 5.48*
   Jesus said to his disciples, 'You, therefore, must be perfect, as your heavenly Father is perfect.'

   RSV

2. *1 John 4.18*
   There is no fear in love, but perfect love casts out fear; for fear has to do with punishment, and whoever fears has not reached perfection in love.

   NRSV

3. *Matthew 19.21*
   Jesus said to the young man 'If you would be perfect, go, sell what you possess and give to the poor, and you will have treasure in heaven; and come, follow me.'

   RSV

4. *1 Peter 1.15–17*
   It is a holy God who has called you, and you too must be holy in all the ordering of your lives; you must be holy, the scripture says, because I am holy.

   K

5. *Colossians 3.12*

As the chosen of God, then, the holy people whom he loves, you are to be clothed in heartfelt compassion, in generosity and humility, gentleness and patience.

NJB

Let us pray:

a) Lord God, come and live in us in the fulness of your power, the reality of your virtues and the perfection of your mysteries. Through Christ our Lord.

b) Almighty God, in giving us your Son, you have given us the source of strength and grace. May we always be faithful to the gifts we receive. Through the same Christ our Lord.

Easter 5 The joy of heaven

When I am totally united to you, there will be no more strain or worry because being filled by you, my life will be complete.

Augustine: *Confessions*, 10

—◁○▷—

1. *Revelation 14.13*
    I John heard a voice from heaven say to me, 'Write down, Happy are those who die in the Lord! Happy indeed, the Spirit says; now they can rest for ever after their work, since their good deeds go with them.'

    JB

2. *John 14.2–3*
    Jesus said to his disciples, 'There are many rooms in my Father's house; if there were not, I should have told you. I am going now to prepare a place for you, and after I have gone and prepared you a place, I shall return to take you with me; so that where I am you may be too.'

    JB

3. *Revelation 21.2, 3–5*
    Then I saw the holy city, new Jerusalem, coming down out of heaven from God ... and I heard a loud voice from the throne saying, 'Behold the dwelling of God is with men. He will dwell with them, and they shall be his people, and God himself will be with them; he will wipe away every tear from their eyes, and death shall be no more, neither shall there be mourning or crying nor pain any more, for the former things have passed away.'

    RSV

4. *1 Corinthians 2.9–11*
It is written, 'What no eye has seen, nor ear heard, nor the human heart conceived, what God has prepared for those who love him' – these things God has revealed to us through the Spirit ...

NRSV

5. *2 Peter 3.13*
We have new heavens and a new earth to look forward to, the dwelling-place of holiness; that is what he has promised.

K

Let us pray:

a) Eternal Father may we die as we desire to live, in your Church, in your faith, and in your holy love. Through Christ our Lord.

b) Heavenly Father, may we live our lives in your presence and come to possess that joy you have prepared for those who love you. Through Christ our Lord.

Easter 6 The communion of saints

(cf. Week 10)

What will be the effect of the complete outpouring of the grace of the Spirit given to us by God? It will transform us into his likeness and make perfect the Father's will in us.

Irenaeus: *Against the Heresies*, Book 5.8

————◄○►————

1. *Ephesians 6.18*
In all your prayer and entreaty keep praying in the Spirit on every possible occasion. Never get tired of staying awake to pray for all God's holy people ...

NJB

2. *1 Corinthians 12.25–26*
There was to be no want of unity in the body [of Christ]; all the different parts of it were to make each other's welfare their common care. If one part is suffering, all the rest suffer with it.

K

3. *Ephesians 2.19–20*
You are fellow citizens with the saints and members of the household of God, built upon the foundation of the apostles and prophets.

RSV

4. *Hebrews 10.24*
Let us be concerned for each other, to stir a response in love and good works.

NJB

5. *Romans 14.7*
    The life and death of each of us has its influence on others;
    if we live, we live for the Lord; and if we die, we die for the
    Lord, so that alive or dead we belong to the Lord.

    JB

Let us pray:

a) Loving Father, grant us time for penance and a peaceful
    death, so that we may love you with all our hearts and
    praise you for ever in the world to come. Through Christ
    our Lord.

b) Eternal God, may we praise you in loving you in whose
    image we are made, and to whom we hope to come at the
    end of our life. Through Christ our Lord.

The Ascension

The Ascension of Christ is also our glorification, for where he has gone the members of his Church hope to follow.

Leo I: Sermon 73

◄○►

1. *Mark 16.19–20*
    The Lord Jesus, after he had spoken to them, was taken up into heaven: there at the right hand of God he took his place, while they, going out, preached everywhere, the Lord working with them and confirming the word by the signs that accompanied it.

    JB

2. *Acts 1.10–12*
    While they were gazing into heaven as he went, behold two men stood by them in white robes, and said, 'Men of Galilee, why do you stand looking into heaven. This Jesus, who was taken up from you into heaven, will come in the same way as you saw him go into heaven.'

    RSV

Let us pray:

a) All powerful God, fill us with your heavenly gifts that we may always be living signs of your kingdom on earth. Through Christ our Lord.

b) Lord God, by the ministry of the angels you guide our way on earth. May we always be prepared to meet you when you should call us from this life. Through Christ our Lord.

Pentecost/Whitsunday

(cf. Weeks 8 and 14)

All who share in the gifts of the Spirit, receive according to the capacity of their own nature, not according to the measure of the power bestowing ... Just as a sunbeam, falling on transparent objects fills them with light and causes them to shine out in brilliance, so too souls which receive the gift of the Spirit become spiritual and send grace to others.

Basil: On the Holy Spirit, 9

———◄◦►———

1. *Romans 5.5*
   Hope does not disappoint us, because God's love has been poured into our hearts through the Holy Spirit who has been given us.

   RSV

2. *1 John 4.11–13*
   If God loved us so much, we too should love each other. No one has ever seen God, but as long as we love each other God remains in us and his love comes to perfection in us.

   NJB

Let us pray:

a) Eternal God, send us your Holy Spirit to strengthen us in our weakness so that we may be ready to do your will. Through Christ our Lord.

b) Almighty God, send forth your Holy Spirit to enlighten our hearts and fill us with the spirit of perfect charity. Through Christ our Lord.

Corpus Christi

(cf. Week 15)

The Eucharist is the same flesh in which our Saviour died and was raised by the Father.

Ignatius of Antioch: Letter to the Smyrnaeans, 6

———◄○►———

1. *John 6. 53–55*

   Jesus said to the crowd, 'Truly, truly I say to you, unless you eat the flesh of the son of man and drink his blood, you have no life in you; he who eats my flesh and drinks my blood has eternal life, and I will raise him up at the last day.'

   RSV

2. *Luke 24.30–32*

   Jesus went in to stay with them. Now while he was with them at table, he took the bread and said the blessing; then he broke it and handed it to them. And their eyes were opened and they recognized him.

   JB

Let us pray:

a) Heavenly Father, you make us one through our communion with your Son, let us also worship his living presence among us in the Blessed Sacrament. Through Christ our Lord.

b) Heavenly Father, as we have received your Son in holy communion, may we live in him as he lives in us. Through the same Christ our Lord.

Occasional Celebrations

Feasts of Our Lady

(cf. Advent 3)

The only-begotten Son of the Father was ... conceived of the Holy Spirit within the womb of his Virgin Mother who brought him into the world without loss of her virginity.

Leo I: Letter to Flavian

—◁◦▷—

1. *Luke 1.46–50*
   Mary said 'My soul proclaims the greatness of the Lord and my spirit exults in God my saviour; because he has looked on his lowly handmaid. Yes, from this day forward all generations will call me blessed, for the Almighty has done great things for me. Holy is his name.'

   JB

2. *John 19.26–28*
   When Jesus saw his mother and the disciple whom he loved standing beside her, he said to his mother, 'Woman, here is your son.' Then he said to the disciple, 'Here is your mother'. And from that hour the disciple took her into his own home.

   NRSV

Let us pray:

a) Eternal Father, may we seek the intercession of Mary who was found worthy to be the mother of our Saviour. Through Christ our Lord.

b) Almighty God, through the intercession of Mary who stood by the cross of your Son may we be strengthened in our sufferings and come to share in your glory. Through Christ our Lord.

Feasts of Martyrs

Martyrdom means bearing witness to God. Everyone who wants to know God with his whole heart and keeps his commandments is in fact a martyr, because he is bearing witness either by his life or by his words.

Clement of Alexandria: Miscellaneous Studies, 4

————◄o►————

1. *Matthew 5.10–13*
   'Happy are those who are persecuted in the cause of right; theirs is the kingdom of heaven. Happy are you when people abuse you and persecute you and speak all kinds of calumnly against you on my account. Rejoice and be glad, for your reward will be great in heaven.

   JB

2. *John 12.24*
   Jesus said to his disciples, 'Truly, truly, I say to you, unless a grain of wheat falls into the earth and dies, it remains alone; but if it dies, it bears much fruit. He who loves his life loses it, and he who hates his life in this world, will keep it for eternal life.'

   RSV

Let us pray:

a) Merciful God, you see our weakness when we fall. Restore us by your love and the example of your holy martyr N. Through Christ our Lord.

b) Heavenly Father, may we who celebrate the feast of your martyr N. be strengthened by his/her witness to live our lives in your presence. Through Christ our Lord.

Feasts of Saints

(cf. Lent 4)

There is a crown for those who, in times of persecution fight the good fight; there is a crown too for those who in peacetime remain true to their conscience.

Cyprian: *Letter to Fortunatus*

————◁◦▷————

1. *John 17.14–17*
Jesus raised his eyes to heaven and said, '... I passed your word on to them, and the world hated them, because they belong to the world no more than I belong to the world. I am not asking you to remove them from the world, but to protect them from the evil one.'

JB

2. *Hebrews 12.1–14*
Since we are surrounded by so great a cloud of witnesses, let us also lay aside every weight and the sin that clings so closely, and let us run with perseverance the race that is set before us, looking to Jesus the pioneer and perfecter of our faith, who for the sake of the joy that was set before him, endured the cross, disregarding its shame, and has taken his seat at the right hand of the throne of God.

NRSV

Let us pray:

a) Heavenly Father, as we celebrate the festival of your saints on earth, may we also imitate their virtue which made them pleasing to you. Through Christ our Lord.

b) Eternal Father we honour N. for the holiness of his/her life. May we always strive for that perfection which he/she achieved, through his/her powerful intercession. Through Christ our Lord.

116

Funerals

(cf. Week 32)

It is that same providence by which God created us out of nothing, that calls us through death to come to him.

John Chrysostom: *On Providence*, 5

————◄o►————

1. *Wisdom 3.1–4*
   The souls of the virtuous are in the hands of God, no torment shall ever touch them. In the eyes of the unwise, they did appear to die, their going looked like a disaster, their leaving us, like annihilation, but they are in peace.

   JB

2. *1 Corinthians 13.12*
   Now we are seeing a dim reflection in a mirror; but then we shall be seeing face to face. The knowledge that I have now is imperfect; but then I shall know as fully as I am known.

   JB

Let us pray:

a) *(For those who have died suddenly)* Merciful Father, may those you have taken suddenly from us be forgiven all their sins and united forever with you. Through Christ our Lord.

b) Merciful Father, comfort us in our sorrow. Forgive N. whatever sins he/she committed and welcome him/her into your kingdom. Through Christ our Lord.

c) Heavenly Father, as your Son rose from the dead to bring us eternal life, may N. share in the same victory over sin and death and be found worthy to enter into eternal life. Through Christ our Lord.

Notes on Christian Authors

(All who are listed are *saints* unless oherwise mentioned)

AMBROSE (339–397)   Lawyer in the imperial service, chosen to be bishop of Milan in 374. Baptized Augustine of Hippo in 386.

ATHANASIUS (295–373)   Accompanied his bishop to the Council of Nicea and succeeded him to the see of Alexandria in 328. Fought against the errors of Arianism and defended the doctrine of the Incarnation.

AUGUSTINE OF HIPPO (354–430)   Born at Tagaste, North Africa and became a brilliant philosopher. He was converted and baptized by St Ambrose and became bishop of Hippo in 396. He wrote 113 books including the *Confessions*.

BASIL (330–379)   A theologian of distinction. He joined the monastery of Annesi but was promoted to the see of Caesarea in 370. His monastic rule which influenced Benedict is still followed by the Eastern Church.

BENEDICT (480–547)   He was sent to Rome for his studies but became a hermit at Subiaco where a community gathered around him. He established a monastery at Monte Cassino c. 529 and is the Father of Western monasticism.

CAESARIUS OF ARLES (470–543)   He was chosen while a monk at Lerins to be bishop of Arles in 503. He presided over several councils and was an energetic and effective bishop, as we can gauge from those homilies which survive.

CLEMENT I (died c. 100)   The third successor of St Peter and venerated as a martyr. He is patron of many marine associations, including *Trinity House*.

CLEMENT OF ALEXANDRIA (150–215)   Born possibly in Athens but studied in Alexandria where he became the leading philosopher in 211. He is not a saint.

CYPRIAN (200–258)   An advocate and orator before he became a Christian c. 245. He was elected to his home see of Carthage in 248. He was martyred under Valerian for not taking part in pagan worship.

CYRIL OF ALEXANDRIA (380–444)   He became bishop of Alexandria in 412 and took he lead at the council of Ephesus against Nestorius. He is called in the East, the 'Seal of the Fathers' for his theological teaching.

DOROTHEUS OF GAZA (sixth century) He lived at the end of the sixth and the beginning of the seventh centuries, becoming Abbot of his monastery.

GREGORY I (540–604) The first of the sixteen popes of that name, was chief magistrate of Rome and became a monk at 35. A consummate statesman and organizer he was elected pope in 590 and sent Augustine of Canterbury to Britain in 597.

GREGORY OF NAZIANZUS (329–389) A fellow-student with Basil in Athens, also joined him at Annesi. He was ordained bishop of Sasima in 372 and of Constantinople in 380 but resigned soon afterwards.

GREGORY OF NYSSA (335–395) A younger brother of Basil and a professor of Rhetoric. He became bishop of Nyssa in 371 and took a prominent part at the council of Constantinople. His work on the soul and the resurrection was addressed to his sister, St Macrina.

HILARY OF POITIERS (315–367) Born into a rich pagan family, he became a Christian and was elected bishop of his native city in 353. He was exiled for four years to Phrygia by the (Arian) emperor but was reinstated. He is known as the Athansasius of the West.

IGNATIUS OF ANTIOCH (died c. 107) Probably of Syrian origin, was sentenced to death as an old man and wrote his letters on the journey to Rome and martyrdom.

IRENAEUS (130–202) Born in Asia Minor but came to Lyons during the persecution of the Christians by Marcus Aurelius. His knowledge of Eastern and Western theology helped him to denounce Gnosticism.

JEROME (341–420) Born in Dalmatia he studied in Rome and the Near East. He settled eventually in Bethlehem in 386 where he translated the Bible from the original sources into Latin (*The Vulgate*).

JOHN OF THE CROSS (1542–1591) Juan de Yepes was one of the first Carmelites to join Teresa of Avila's reform at Duruelo. He suffered repeatedly for this decision, and removed from office, died in Ubeda.

JOHN CHRYSOSTOM (347–407) The son of a serving officer in the army he joined the clergy of Antioch in 381 with a growing reputation as a preacher. He was elected to the see of

Constantinople in 398 but was banished and died on the journey into exile.

JUSTIN (100–165)   Born at Nablus (Shechem) to a pagan family, he was baptized c. 133 and became a great lay apologist for Christianity. He was denounced for his faith when he was in Rome, and beheaded.

LEO I (died c. 461)   Skilled as a negotiator he was in Gaul when he was elected pope in 440. He exercised a great influence at the council of Chalcedon in 451.

NEWMAN, J. H. (1801–1890)   Nineteenth-century preacher and writer, he became a Catholic in 1845 after a distinguished career at Oxford. He founded the English Oratory and was created Cardinal by Leo XIII in 1879. His cause for canonization is far advanced.

ORIGEN (185–254)   Born in Alexandria became versed in scripture and philosophy and was invited by the bishops to lecture and catechize, settling in Caesarea. He preferred allegory and his theories were often very speculative. He died during the Decian persecution but is not considered a martyr.

TERTULLIAN (160–222)   Probably born at Carthage, was converted to Christianity in 190 but became a Montanist c. 207, won over by its extreme asceticism. Not a saint.

Appendix 1 Additional Prayers

General prayers

I believe (the Apostles' Creed)

I believe in God, the Father almighty, creator of heaven and earth. I believe in Jesus Christ, his only Son, our Lord. He was conceived by the power of the Holy Spirit and born of the Virgin Mary. He suffered under Pontius Pilate, was crucified, died, and was buried. He descended to the dead. On the third day he rose again. He ascended into heaven, and is seated at the right hand of the Father. He will come again to judge the living and the dead. I believe in the Holy Spirit, the holy Catholic Church, the communion of saints, the forgiveness of sins, the resurrection of the body, and the life everlasting. Amen.

Prayer to the Holy Spirit

Come, Holy Spirit, fill the hearts of your faithful and kindle in them the fire of your love. Send forth your Spirit and they shall be created and you shall renew the face of the earth.

Let us pray:
O God you taught the hearts of the faithful by the light of the Holy Spirit; grant that by the gift of the same Spirit, we may be always wise and ever rejoice in his consolation. Through Christ our Lord. Amen.

Act of faith

My God, I believe in you and all that your Church teaches, because you have said it, and your word is true.

Act of hope

My God, I hope in you, for grace and for glory, because of your promises, your mercy and your power.

Appendix 1

Act of charity

God, because you are so good, I love you with all my heart, and for your sake, I love my neighbour as myself.

Act of contrition

O my God, because you are so good, I am very sorry that I have sinned against you and by the help of your grace I will not sin again.

Prayers during the day

Act of the presence of God (before prayer)

My God, I believe you are here, that you see me and you know me. I adore you with profound reverence and I ask pardon for my sins. Help me to make this time of prayer fruitful.

Prayer before work or study

Almighty God, be the beginning and end of all we do and say. Prompt our actions with your grace and complete them with your all powerful help. Through Christ Our Lord. Amen.

Prayers of dedication

O God, to whom every heart is open, every desire known and from whom no secrets are hidden; purify the thoughts of our hearts by the inspiration of your Holy Spirit, that we may perfectly love you, and worthily praise your holy name. Through Christ our Lord. Amen.

To the Father, King of ages who is immortal, invisible, the one and only God, be honour and glory for ever and ever. Amen.

Eternal God, who are the light of the minds that know you, the joy of the hearts that love you, and the strength of the wills that serve you, grant us so to know you that we may truly love you, and so to love you that we may truly serve you, whom to serve is perfect freedom. (St Augustine)

Prayers to the Blessed Virgin Mary

Hail Holy Queen

Hail Holy Queen, mother of mercy; hail our life, our sweetness, and our hope! To thee do we cry, poor banished children of Eve; to thee do we send up our sighs, mourning and weeping in this vale of tears. Turn then, most gracious advocate, thine eyes of mercy towards us; and after this our exile, show unto us the blessed fruit of thy womb, Jesus. O clement, O loving, O sweet Virgin Mary.
Pray for us, O holy Mother of God
That we may be made worthy of the promises of Christ.

The Memorare

Remember, O most loving Virgin Mary, that it is a thing unheard of, that anyone ever had recourse to your protection, implored your help, or sought your intercession, and was left forsaken. Filled therefore with confidence in your goodness I fly to you, O Mother, Virgin of virgins. To you I come, before you I stand, a sorrowful sinner. Despise not my poor words, O Mother of the Word of God, but graciously hear and grant my prayer.

Prayer for Our Lady's protection

We fly to thy patronage, O holy Mother of God; despise not our petitions in our necessities, but deliver us always from all dangers, O glorious and blessed Virgin.

The Angelus (The angel's greeting to Mary at Nazareth)

The angel of the Lord declared unto Mary
R/ And she conceived by the Holy Spirit. Hail Mary ...

Behold the handmaid of the Lord
R/ Be it done to me according to your word. Hail Mary ...

The Word was made flesh
R/ And dwelt among us. Hail Mary ...

Pray for us, O holy Mother of God
R/ That we may be made worthy of the promises of Christ

Let us pray:
Pour forth, we beseech you, O Lord, your grace into our hearts, that we to whom the Incarnation of Christ your Son was made known by the message of an angel, may, by his Passion and Cross, be brought to the glory of his resurrection. Through Christ Our Lord. Amen.

Regina Caeli (Queen of Heaven)
(recited in place of the Angelus during Eastertide)

Queen of heaven, rejoice! Alleluia.
For he whom you merited to bear, Alleluia.
Has risen, as he said, Alleluia.
Pray for us to God. Alleluia.

V. Rejoice and be glad, O Virgin Mary, Alleluia.
R/ For the Lord has risen indeed. Alleluia.

Let us pray:
O God, who through the resurrection of your Son,
Our Lord Jesus Christ, willed to fill the world with joy,
grant, we beseech you, that through his Virgin Mother,
Mary, we may come to the joys of everlasting life.
Through the same Christ Our Lord. Amen.

Prayers for those who have died

Eternal Rest grant to them, O Lord
And let perpetual light shine upon them.
May they rest in peace. Amen.

May the souls of the faithful departed, through the mercy of God rest in peace. Amen.

The De Profundis (Psalm 130)

Out of the depth, I have cried to you, O Lord.
Lord hear my voice.

Let your ears be attentive.
To the voice of my supplication.
If you, O Lord, shall observe iniquities,
Lord, who shall endure it?
For with you there is merciful forgiveness;
And by reason of your law, I have waited for you, O Lord.
My soul has relied on his word;
My soul has hoped in the Lord
From the morning watch even until night
Let Israel hope in the Lord
Because with the Lord there is mercy
And with him plentiful redemption.
And He shall redeem Israel
from all his iniquities.

Prayer for all the Holy Souls

O God, the creator and redeemer of all the faithful, grant to the souls of your servants departed the remission of all their sins, that through our pious supplication they may obtain that pardon which they have always desired; who live and reign for ever and ever. Amen.

Prayer for a happy death

O Lord, support us all the day long until the shadows lengthen and the evening comes and the busy world is hushed and the fever of life is over, and our work is done. Then, Lord, in your mercy, grant us a safe lodging, a holy rest, and peace at the last. Amen.

Cardinal Newman

May the Lord bless us, may he keep us from all evil and bring us to life everlasting. Amen.

Appendix 2

Index to paragraphs in the Catechism of the Catholic Church

Subject Index

Subject index